Cultures
of Change
Social Atoms
and Electronic Lives

Generalitat de Catalunya
Departament de Cultura
i Mitjans de Comunicació

ACTAR

_RTS S_NT_ MÒNIC_

SIXTH FRAMEWORK
PROGRAMME

Edition
Actar and Arts Santa Mònica

Texts © the authors
Translations © the translators
This edition © Actar/Arts Santa Mònica-
Ministry of Culture and the Media,
Government of Catalonia

Distributed by
ACTAR D
Roca i Batlle, 2
08023 Barcelona
Tel.: +34 93 417 49 93
Fax: +34 93 418 67 07
office@actar-d.com
www.actar-d.com

Bookshops of Government of Catalonia
www.gencat.cat/publicacions

ISBN
978-84-92861-14-9
(Actar)
78-84-393-8191-4
(Arts Santa Mònica)

Dipòsit Legal
B-44314-2009

Arts Santa Mònica
La Rambla, 7
08002 Barcelona
Tel.: +34 93 316 28 10
www.artssantamonica.cat

Actar
Barcelona/New York
www.actar.com

Arts Santa Mònica gratefully acknowledges the support of the Corporació Catalana de Mitjans Audiovisuals, of *La Vanguardia*, *Vilaweb* and *Mau Mau* as collaborating media, and of the Fundació Bosch i Gimpera of the Universitat de Barcelona, and the INCOM of the Universitat Autònoma de Barcelona as collaborating academic institutions.

EXHIBITION
Curators
Josep Perelló and Pau Alsina with the assistance of Irma Vilà
Exhibition design
pocaa
Coordination Arts Santa Mònica
Fina Duran and Lurdes Ibarz
Acknowledgements
Alex Adriaansens, Ramon Balagué, Jasmina Bolfek-Radovani, Michele Catanzaro, EventLab UB, Matthew Fuller, Celia Lury, Vicente Matallana, Pere Monràs, Núria Sentís, Carles Tardío, Oriol Vallès, YProductions.

Arts Santa Mònica , Barcelona
From 11 December 2009 to 28 February 2010

BOOK
Edited by **Gennaro Ascione, Cinta Massip and Josep Perelló**
Graphic design
Cèlia Costa@ Actar Pro
Digital production
Oriol Rigat @ Actar Pro

Translations from Catalan
Graham Thomson

Impressió
Ingoprint SA

A production of Arts Santa Mònica – Ministry of Culture and the Media of the Government of Catalonia. With collaboration of A Topological Approach to Cultural Dynamics (NEST PathFinder under Sixth Framework Programme of the European Union), Goldsmiths - University of London, Media Studies - Universiteit van Amsterdam, Universitat de Barcelona, Advanced Hardware Architectures - Universitat Politècnica de Catalunya, Neàpolis, Universitat Oberta de Catalunya and BEEP.

Illuminations in the Night of the Hyperworld

Vicenç Altaió
Director of Arts Santa Mònica

Welcome to the Laboratory at Arts Santa Mònica, a centre without a centre as a reflection of a culture that is complex in points of view and verb tenses; a place of places to break through the boundaries that separate the disciplines of knowledge, the inside and the outside, and open up to collision and exchange. What we offer is an environment for joint working, a space to learn in, a living laboratory. In not differentiating science and art, memory and technology, we create becoming with a performative concurrence.

Humanity now and always has lived in the midst of change and, at times, mutation. We accept the flow of things and give death its place in the natural cycle. In living with a critical consciousness attentive to mutation, we learn from radically fresh sensations, anticipations and feelings of pleasure and understanding: we are atoms in motion before art objects.

This ultramodern exhibition — an impulse towards the There Ahead — emerges from the There Beyond, because nothing comes from nothing. In the task of uniting ideas, I see *Cultures of Change* as recovering the concepts of atom and pleasure formulated by Democritus, and of atoms and the void re-elaborated by Epicurus and beautifully embodied in Lucretius' poem *De Rerum Natura*. It offers us a wealth of "new words" and "new uses" derived from analogies that experimental science and art have combined to construct together: from an environment-sensitive sculptural group to three-dimensional drawings made from nets. Open to the novel and the fantastic, these real simulations affect our mental representations and create a wholly new speculative culture and an understanding with practical instrumental quality in construction: Arts of Art.

With *Cultures of Change*, the first exhibition conceived by the Laboratory at Arts Santa Mònica, we have set out to accommodate a number of experimental simulations of a practical, living imaginary in constant mutation. Projects and programmes conceived in the Europe of thought and innovation. From our local universities we have included works of art and science and the Internet (UOC), robotics and artificial intelligence (UPC) and physics and scientific communication (UB). Coming from research centres and academia, these works produced jointly and equally by scientists, designers, artists and technologists find here, in the space of arts-science-communication, a crossroads between exercise and aesthetics, experience and enjoyment, anticipation and communication. In this way, in the shift from the material society to the society of readily available knowledge and information, the experiment takes on the value of shared collective social experience.

Social Atoms and Electronic Lives

Josep Perelló

How can pollen particles suspended in water remain in never-ending motion, in an agitation, an erratic displacement that "[arises] neither from currents in the Fluid, or from its gradual evaporation, but [belongs] to the particle itself?" This was the question the Scottish botanist Robert Brown, who was studying the mechanisms involved in the pollination of the flower *Clarkia pulchella*, asked himself in 1827.

What we know as Brownian motion is an engine that runs without fuel. It disperses particles: in botanical terms, it pollinates and germinates. It is the random movement that prevented Brown's pollen grains from settling at the bottom of the dish. In doing so it defies and overcomes the force of gravity, that great pillar of Newtonian physics, the interaction that supposedly governs our entire existence.

Brown replicated his experimental observation with pollen from other plant species and with other vegetable matter, but if he was at any point tempted to imagine he had found the pulse, the very essence of life, he avoided that temptation. Some years previously, in 1785, Jan Ingenhousz had described the same irregular movement in coal dust, an inanimate material, on the surface of liquid alcohol. More tantalizing still, back in the first century BC, the Roman philosopher Lucretius in *De Rerum Natura* had made a similar observation:

"Observe what happens when sunbeams are admitted into a building and shed light on its shadowy places. You will see a multitude of tiny particles mingling in a multitude of ways... their dancing is an actual indication of underlying movements of matter that are hidden from our sight... It originates with the atoms which move of themselves [i.e. spontaneously]. Then those small compound bodies that are least removed from the impetus of the atoms are set in motion by the impact of their invisible blows and in turn cannon against slightly larger bodies. So the movement mounts up from the atoms and gradually emerges to the level of our senses, so that those bodies are in motion that we see in sunbeams, moved by blows that remain invisible."

The fact is that we can credit Brown, Ingenhousz and Lucretius, who did not have the powerful microscopes that allow us today to probe even the Nanoscale, with the first proofs of the existence of atoms — tiny "fundamental" particles in continual collision with their neighbours. The sum of these collisions is a dance abounding in irregularities, in which a virtually infinite number of individually insignificant entities are capable of countering the mighty force of gravity itself.

In 1905, Albert Einstein added his grain of sand by corroborating the atomic premise. The great physicist provided a mathematical account of Brownian motion in terms of probability and chance to calculate the trajectory of an individual particle. Statistical Physics thus builds the bridge between the micro and macro. Observations are merely statistical averages of the random variability of each atom, but taken overall, atoms conform to well-established certainties, with macroscopic observables such as temperature and pressure.

This whole disquisition on uncertainty at the atomic level continues to run comfortably on top of macroscopic determinism. We can see its validity in the case of systems in equilibrium: in other words, stable, homogeneous structures, without changes of temperature, with no heat flows between liquid and ambient air, with no exchange of matter or energy. Clearly, however, if we are dealing with living organisms, the hypotheses are far from being acceptable premises.

Out of Equillibrium and Spontaneous Order

Still within the realms of equilibrium and stability, the first person to expose the fragility of Newtonian determinism was Henri Poincaré, around 1900, with specific reference to the sun-earth-moon system, which interacts gravitationally. It is impossible to work out with exactitude in mathematical terms a system with even as many as three bodies. At the other extreme, in weather, probably the best-known chaotic system, we find millions of atoms of the most diverse natures interacting strongly outside of any kind of imaginable balance. In the famous butterfly effect associated with the name of Edward Lorenz the non-linearities of interacting particles are capable of causing dramatic changes in the weather, for example, as a result of almost imperceptible movements such as innocent beating of a butterfly's wings in the Amazon rain forest.

In the mid twentieth century, Lorenz tried to grab order in the chaos of meteorology in diagrammatic form, using maps representing both the position and the speed of the particles. This rendering translates the world to a larger space than the one we perceive in order to identify regularities that will make it intelligible. The necessary observation also call for a global perspective, because we cannot grasp these structures simply by carefully plotting the course of a particle.

For a classic instance of creation of structures through randomness, consider the following mechanism. A particle moves from right to left at a random altitude, and if it encounters another particle on its way the two join up. This process is repeated countless times, and the resulting form is an agglomeration or cluster of branching particles which spread out in all directions like the veins and arteries of the circulatory system, the roots and branches of a tree, the cracks in a sheet of glass or a satellite picture of a river. Structures of this kind, known as fractals, are common to a great diversity of phenomena. They have the distinctive property of presenting the same form and appearance whether we are looking at a larger or smaller subdivision of their ramifications or the structure in its entirety.

Another model is a network of springs connected together in a mesh or lattice mode with a particle of a certain mass at each node. Each particle oscillates in response to the vibrating of the springs which in turn transmit the oscillations to adjacent objects. Think of a small number of connected particles and you will probably envisage a chaotic oscillatory dynamic. But now imagine hundreds, thousands or millions of vibrating particles and it becomes increasingly possible for all the particles to synchronize and beat in unison. From the microscopic stratum we find ourselves looking at the emergence of an orderly global dynamic. The idea is currently being applied to analyse the self-organization of a mass of heart cells that end up beating at the same rhythm, millions of neurons being activated at the same time and bringing on an attack of epilepsy, a community of fireflies in an American forest all flashing on and off at the same time or, in a more prosaic situation, the synchronization of the applause from a theatre audience. As I said, we are talking about living organisms. Biomedicine, which studies the growth and division of cells, also observes that a limited number of very simple rules of development is sufficient to create highly sophisticated living systems at the macroscopic level.

Social Atoms, Complexity Theory and Electronic Lives

All of these examples, metaphors models and analogies invite us to look beyond specific individual disciplines of knowledge. Brownian motion was identified by a botanist, taken up by physicists and in fact also has applications in economics. In 1900, five years before Einstein tackled it, Louis Bachelier had already presented the mathematical model that set out to explain the erratic movement not of atoms but of share prices on the Paris stock exchange. For Bachelier, the brokers were the liquid medium and the grains of pollen the stocks, which receive impacts that cause their value to go up or down. The random path proposed by the theory served for the economy and is also currently applied in fields such as biology, chemistry, geology and sociology, among others. And to take it a step further, Benoît Mandelbrot first studied the fractal structures we mentioned above not to study physical systems but to interpret variations in the price of cotton.

Can individuals and society be read in the same way as erratic grains of pollen suspended in a liquid? Does it make sense to speak of a channel through which ideas can circulate from one field of knowledge to another? Does this communication serve to enhance our understanding of the world? It would be risky to give an unconditional "yes" to these questions, but it would be equally wrong to reject this transdisciplinary vision. The interactions may be of a different nature, but that matters little in the so-called theory of complexity. Analysis of complex systems (the word "complex" comes from the Latin root *plexus* meaning to be interwoven) overwhelmingly places the emphasis on relationships: what is related to what. These relationships take on an abstract profile that is largely indifferent to their nature as such, be it gravitational, electrical or personal affinity. The theory of complexity gives rise to the visualization of complex networks of interaction and chaos maps, and also to the construction of dynamic models — with or without chance component — whose non-linear fractal properties enable them to accommodate the butterfly effect.

In addition, dialogue between disciplines and the adoption of a global perspective on certain problems are essential in the tumultuous world of today. This is most clearly the case in the fight against climate change, where the future of humanity itself is at stake. Combating the greenhouse effect involves a technological challenge, a profound rethinking of our economic and political models and a heightening of social awareness in which art, too, has a role to play alongside scientists of all kinds — climatologists, biologists, experts in new energy sources and others. None of these by themselves can resolve the problem, which requires the cooperation and collaboration of all.

Cultures of Change

The real change in the study of social dynamics in the broadest possible sense has come about thanks to the new information technologies. There are now digital records of almost everything, almost everywhere. For example, financial markets store all of the transactions and all of the price variations generated second by second, even recording the names of the agents who handle the bids to buy and sell stocks and shares. What is monitored here is a world of social atoms in continuous interaction. The same is true of mobile phone networks, which keep permanent track of us and at the same time allow us to trace patterns of behaviour in human communication and the geography of people's daily movements. The social networks, in turn, seek to forge friendships, while offering the scientist an excellent database for studying the mechanisms that underlie personal affinities or the transmission of certain items of news suppressed by other, conventional channels. And all the time the powerful computers we have today are busy simulating and further evolving this world of springs, of sticky particles or any other model with a simple mechanics but an infinite number of iterations.

So, after all that, what do we see? What do we want to see thanks to this transfer of knowledge based on the physics of atoms? We want to see relationships, the dynamics rooted in microscopic behaviour that give rise to large-scale structures and patterns. Of course, it would be absurd to imagine that the communities we study are composed of identical atoms as in physics. Heterogeneity, diversity and the limitations of quantification of even our best science and technology are significant factors here. Nor should we believe that physics can do all this on its own. Further progress depends the involvement of disciplines such as economics, psychology, anthropology and sociology. Similarly, it is surely symptomatic that so much of today's electronics — the truly new contemporary technology — is developing warm epithelial tissue and a breath that is more and more human.

The NEST PathFinder initiative A Topological Approach to Cultural Dynamics, part of the European Commission's 6th Framework Programme, illustrates all these confluences of thought, with all their strengths and all their weaknesses. Some of those involved have contributed to this book. Taken all together, this collection of texts gives us a snapshot, inevitably partial though it is, of this initiative. It outlines this cultural change. It describes the horizontal shifts more or less imposed on academic cultures by the hectic modern world. It shows how the toughest science and technology are moving closer to the culture of the arts and humanities.

Brown's mechanisms of pollination and germination are a metaphor and a gateway, an invitation to imagine a cross-fertilization between branches of knowledge capable of nurturing a renewed humanism.

Omnes et Singulatim:

Surviving Singularities, Totalities and Complexities

Pau Alsina

Never before have we had such so much information at our disposal. But having information is not necessarily the same as having knowledge. We know they are different things that often need one another. Nowadays, thanks to the information and communication technologies, we can access and store huge amounts of data and information of every kind from everywhere. But the challenge is not only quantitative, it is also qualitative, and so we try to obtain information that is both relevant and accurate. How do we establish quality and significance? The frameworks within which relevance and accuracy are constructed are central to the impulse to obtain, store and process data. How do we construct these frameworks? What do they help us look for? What are they?

Information and communication technologies, with their potential for processing, calculating, visualizing, monitoring, quantifying and distributing data, provide us with both a new vision of the world and new experiences to explore. The challenges consist precisely in knowing how to use all of this potential deriving from the appropriate frameworks, pointing in the right directions so as to generate helpful knowledge that seems likely to bring about changes for the better in our culture and the world. So-called Complex Systems Theory seeks to explain this whole phenomenon on a hard scientific basis in terms of models that assume properties such as non-linearity, self-organization, emergence, feedback, heterogeneity and uncertainty.

Living with this potential treatment of singularities that construct highly complex totalities represents a challenge that the so-called sciences of complexity have embraced since their inception. These complex systems are composed of interconnected parts which, taken as a whole, possess properties that are not found in the individual component parts. Deciphering these properties, these behaviours intrinsic to complex systems is a task that has come to include the mathematical sciences and also the natural and social sciences, and has helped to generate a series of interdisciplinary specializations, ranging from cybernetics to theories of complexity.

Knowledge thus generated has numerous and extremely diverse fields of application, and represents a highly significant contribution to society as a whole, a contribution that many have sought to highlight by noting that it represents a change of paradigm in process, giving rise to ontological and above all epistemological shifts of the first magnitude. The present exhibition sets out to study, from a highly multidisciplinary perspective, the transformational impact that all of these conceptual and technological developments are having on cultural and social dynamics.

The aim was therefore to show, on the one hand, how sciences have progressed in their attempts to describe and explain complex phenomena and, on the other hand, how the technologies have given additional impetus to this knowledge both by shifting the boundaries of the questions addressed and by posing new questions by way of a wide range of applications, some of them experimental, others well established in our culture. To this end, along our route, we find documentary pieces reflecting the diversity of perspectives and opinions about these changes we are witnessing, and experimental pieces that are especially useful for an understanding of the magnitude of the associated ideas, and other pieces that are essentially poetic in their attempt to capture the significance of the cultural and human potential inherent in the new theorizations and ongoing applications.

The itinerary starts out from the purest abstraction — where mathematics makes it possible to represent this complexity with its formulas, detecting and revealing hidden patterns — and then moves on to the model-ling of this complexity — producing simplified abstractions in which either computation or simulation or quantification or parameterization play a cru-cial role — and finally comes to the various applications of these complex systems in culture and society, which give rise to a whole new set of possi-bilities with a diversity of social, cultural and artistic facets to be explored.

The key element in these theoretical abstractions that describe so-cial dynamics is their interaction and co-evolution with the environment. Atoms borrowed from physics take on here a manifestly social character, as robotics, electronic circuitry and the latest technological gadgets move ever closer to incorporating human particularities. The exhibition invites us to experience all these ideas at first hand while, at the same time, it provides specialist academic information about this topic in an academic environment that aims to make it accessible and readily understandable.

Today we can inquire into the characteristic patterns and mecha-nisms of the dynamics of complex phenomena, the illuminating potential of complexity by means of its adequate representation and the need for simplifying models or analogies and their potential as explanatory meta-phors. This exhibition aims to help making us more aware of the social and cultural significance of these advances, their potential and the way they change the image we have of the world, taking us from the change of cul-tures to cultures of change.

Visualization

History and Memory in the Digital Era

Alex Adriaansens

Our understanding of past, present and future is closely linked to the way we organize and process information with electronic media and how we retrieve knowledge and meaning out of these processes.

In contemporary archival practices it is not just the individual data that are being stored in databases. The relationships and correlations between the various data are now also being stored, by using "Meta-Data." Meta-Data (also known as "tags") are data that describe and categorize other data. Meta-Data as means for ordering, hierarchizing, streamlining and evaluating have become increasingly important as social, political and economical instruments in an informational sphere that, for a long time, was considered as being value-free.

In various contemporary views "the archive" has proved to be a strong metaphor. The human body has become a genetic archive itself, now that it has been digitally opened up in the *Human Genome Project*. Our language is an archive of meanings that can be unlocked by philological methods. It teaches us who we are and where we come from. The unconscious is an archive of all the traumatic experiences that define our identity. History is a database from which facts can be arbitrarily retrieved, and now it lacks one big unifying story.

Archives no longer just contain our past for inspection by historians and other researchers. We are permanently living in archives: all the sites we visit on the Internet are logged by our search engines and are monitored by mostly illegal spy bots who are installed in our machines without us knowing about it. All our shopping is registered by our supermarkets. On the basis of such archives the policies for the future are being planned.

Behind almost every activity in the hard, material world nowadays hides an immaterial archive. We are living in the world's online archive or, more to the point, we are living in the world-as-archive, as a constellation of databases all connected with each other by a global network of computers: the Internet.

Because archives are continuously available and accessible, they have become an essential factor for acting and interacting in the present. One could even say that archives have become crucial in how the present is created and reflected upon.

Information isn't power, but knowledge is. Knowledge is tagged, or intelligently grouped and combined, information. Knowledge is the result of the (open or concealed, private or public, controllable or associative) knowledge management of data and data clusters.

Acting and interacting puts forward the question of how our media world is structured and is structuring itself through interaction. It puts forward the question of how open or closed media systems are and how interaction comes about, how it is designed or spontaneously emerging in technical media networks as well as in biological, social and cultural systems and eventually leading to variation and diversity.

In a world dominated by an omnipresence of media and telecommunications networks, we are confronted with changing social, cultural and political relations. The way we are used to socially or politically act and interact, how interaction comes about, and what social, cultural, artistic or political forms they generate is an essential part of how media affect and shape our contemporary social, cultural and political experiences.

Interaction is a characteristic of every living being. Interaction is the formation of connections and networks, and the bringing about of organization, structure and memory through interplay within them. Interaction changes bodies and objects. Interaction is not a morphing of existing structures but adding information to them, and therefore the formation of thoughts and structures.

To better understand interaction within and between networks, and the social, cultural and artistic forms it generates, we must analyze the principles according to which it works. In biological networks, structures emerge spontaneously through self-organization on the basis of interactions which affect each other. Technological networks, by contrast, are formal and stringently controlled. Social and cultural interaction, however, does not fit into this binary division: it is hybrid and continually yields surprising outcomes, even though strict control functions are at play at the same time. Flexibility and temporality, expressed in media networks, are therefore key terms when we talk about interaction in fields such as culture, the social sphere and other domains.

Sky Ear
& Open Burble

Usman Haque

"Sky Ear"

The story of Sky Ear begins in my studio in Japan in 2000. I was wandering around trying to find good reception on my mobile phone. I started to imagine the undulating qualities of an invisible topography that surrounded me: the varying electromagnetic fields (EMF) that are present everywhere and that guided me to certain parts of the room in order to use my phone.

I realised that these intangible phenomena affect the way we related to space and to each other in much the same way that traditional architectural elements do — they make us move to certain parts of a building, they condition the movements we make and how we make them and, through devices like mobile phones, they have a direct impact on the way we associate with other people. Apart from issues arising out of being in contact virtually anywhere, anytime, the mobile technologies through which we conduct our daily lives have made us far more aware of the electromagnetic environment that envelops us.

We are concerned about the health effects of electromagnetic radiation (from power lines or mobile phone handsets) and this has further spatial implications. Yet these waves often exist as natural phenomena in the form of radio waves emanating from distant stars, gamma rays coming from elements here on earth or even electrical waves from inside our own skulls. Humans have only recently begun contributing to the cacophony with their pagers, medical devices, televisions broadcasts and mobile phones.

With Sky Ear, I wanted to give form to this space, to make visible the invisible. I planned to create a large structure, of about 30m in diameter, that would float up into the sky sampling the electromagnetic environment as it moved, and changing colours as it encountered different qualities of space. I realised that by embedding mobile phones inside the cloud and then calling into them, one could actually change the local EMF to create different patterns of response.

The production design was a carbon fibre frame consisting of 37 circles joined to form a non-rigid structure to which 1000 extra-large helium balloons are attached. The balloons function both as buoyancy/flotation devices and as diffusers for the 6 ultra-bright LED (which mix to make millions of colours) controlled by individual microcontrollers inside each balloon. The balloons can communicate with each other via infra-red; this allows them to send signals to create larger patterns across the entire Sky Ear cloud.

As visitors call into the different mobile phones in the cloud, they listen to the distant electromagnetic sounds of the sky (called whistlers and spherics, which are the audible equivalent of the Aurora Borealis). Their mobile phone calls change the local electromagnetic topography and cause disturbances in the EMF inside the cloud that alters the glow intensity and colour of that part of the balloon cloud.

Feedback within the sensor network creates ripples of light reminiscent of rumbling thunder and flashes of lightning.

Sky Ear. David Rothschild Photography 2004

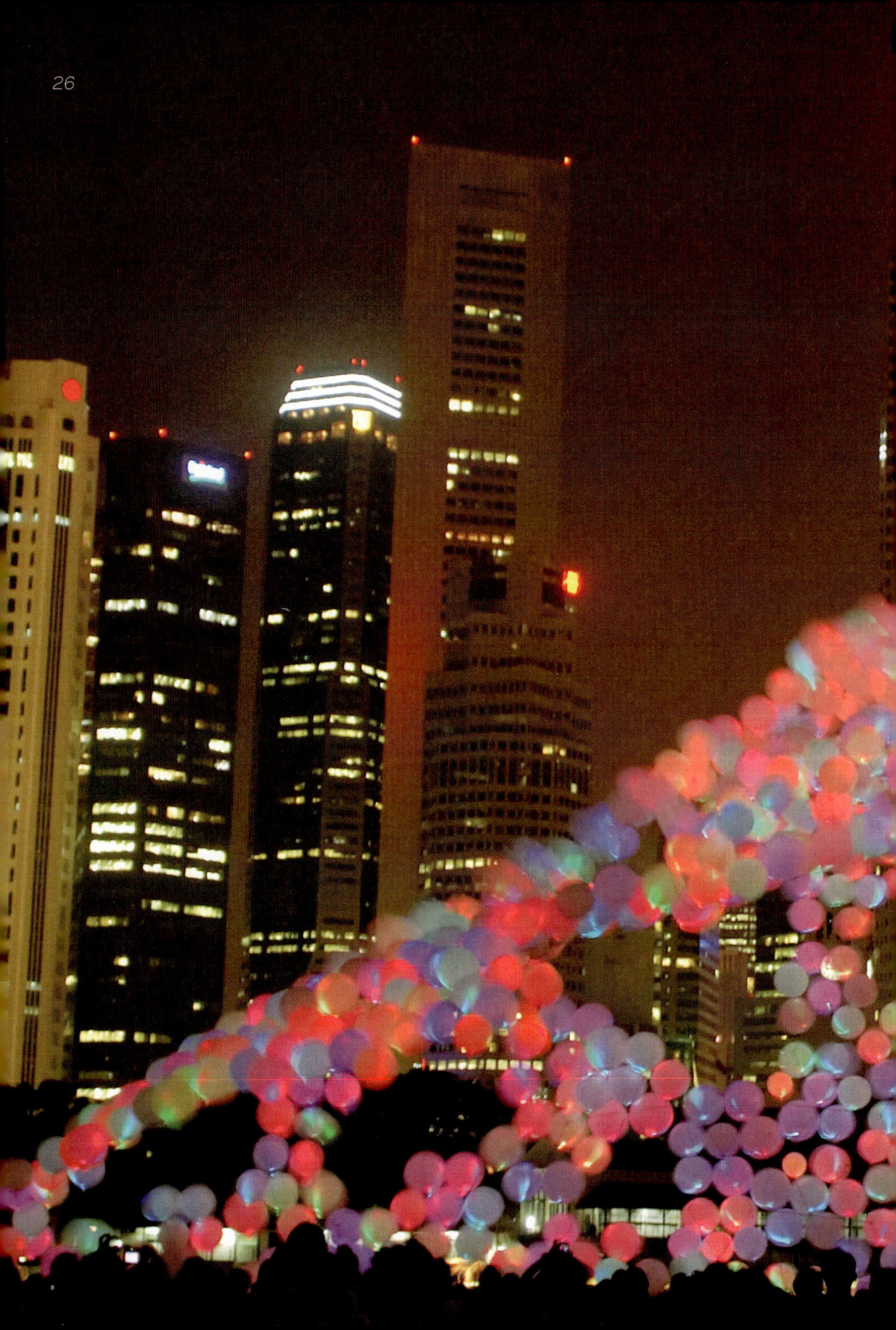

"Open Burble"

Open Burble was motivated by vary interests: to explore what I call the "granularities of participation." I created the Burble as a modular framework that could be assembled by non-specialist members of the public: the idea was to provide a kit-of-parts that people (who don't normally consider themselves designers) could come together to produce something so large that it could compete visually at an urban scale: even if just for one night, they could contribute to their urban context at the scale of a 15-storey building.

The Burble is constructed from a set of 140 modular and configurable carbon-fibre units approx. 2m in diameter. Each unit is supported by 7 extra-large helium balloons (for a total of about 1000 individual pixels) which contain sensors, LEDs and microcontrollers (the same as in Sky Ear), enabling balloons and units to co-ordinate and create patterns of colour that ripple up towards the sky.

Just as the participants are the composers of the Burble's tall form, so too are they the ones to control it. They hold on to it using handles with which they may position the Burble as they like. They may curve in on themselves, or pull it in a straight line — the form is a combination of the crowd's desires and the impact of wind currents varying throughout the height of the Burble.

People have a number of different ways of participating in the project (i.e. different "granularities" or "resolutions" or "commitments" to the project): (a) they might be involved at the design stage, creating patterns and shapes from the individual modular components, which they will later be able to recognise in the final structure; (b) they might take part in the assembly process; (c) they might control, position and manipulate the 15-storey Burble once it's finally afloat — the way that the colours bleed across the surface depends entirely on how the Burble was designed and configured in the first place; (d) or they might do all of the above.

The point is that different people, at different times, will have different desires, interests, skill levels, or commitment to contribute to any public project and I wanted to explore how to provide as much openness at different levels as possible.

The project is considered successful when one of the participants points at the structure and says "that's mine!"...

Evolution of Technology Innovation Networks

Sergi Valverde

This year we are celebrating the 200th anniversary of the birth of Charles Darwin and the 150th anniversary of the publication of his masterpiece The Origin of Species (1859), a crucial milestone in our comprehension of the evolutionary forces shaping nature. Darwin explained life as the outcome of strong competition between species, which struggle for survival in a resource-limited environment. As a result of natural selection forces, organisms become more and more different over many generations. At some moment, these descendant organisms are so different from their ancestry that we can no longer group them under the same rubric and then, a new species is born (i.e., speciation).

Evolutionary theory is both a very elegant and powerful framework. It is so attractive, that researchers from outside biology have drawn parallels between their own topic of study (in particular, sociological and economic studies) and the principles of evolutionary theory. Indeed, evolution has deeply transformed the scientifc thought and many intellectual fields. However, evolutionary theory has some limitations and it does not readily apply to every non- biological process of change. Can we understand the pattern of variation and the diversity of human inventions using a Darwinian approach? In a related approach, archeologists, linguists and anthropologists have studied the evolution of cultural diversity using phylogenetic trees.[1] These trees describe the past relationships between cultures, languages or artifacts, assuming that cultural traits evolve by descent with modifcation. Similarly, biological phylogenetic trees (or evolutionary trees) show the evolutionary relationships between different species that are believed to have a common ancestor. A node in a phylogenetic tree represents the most common ancestor of a set of descendant nodes, which are linked to their ancestor through an edge.

The study of cultural diversity from an evolutionary perspective offers many advantages but some interesting challenges as well. At best, the phylogenetic tree is a hypothesis about how culture evolves under certain assumptions that might not hold for some cases. For example, how tree-like is cultural evolution? Recently, we have explored this issue with the patent citation network[2] from the United States Patent and Trademark Office (USPTO). This large database comprises some 3 million patents and all the citations from one patent to all the (related) preceding inventions (see figure). From this patent citation network, we can trace the sequence of intermediate steps towards a particular invention. Unlike phylogenetic trees, the patent network is not tree-like. We can clearly appreciate that the path to invention can be quite complex: there is vertical, horizontal and oblique inheritance and borrowing is widespread. Nature is far more limited when evolving organisms.

In the future, the analysis of this network will enable a more detailed understanding of the differences between natural and artificial evolution and the specific mechanisms underlying technological innovation. In addition, the patent citation networks can help us to understand the pattern of technology adoption in our society and across companies and industrial fields. Recent studies suggest the spread of technological innovations can be described by population contagion models[3], which were suitably adapted from epidemiology to the dynamics of invention. Here, the patent citation network enables the unambiguous identification of what inventions have been preceded by other ancestor inventions and to reconstruct the spread of innovations through time.

FIG. 1

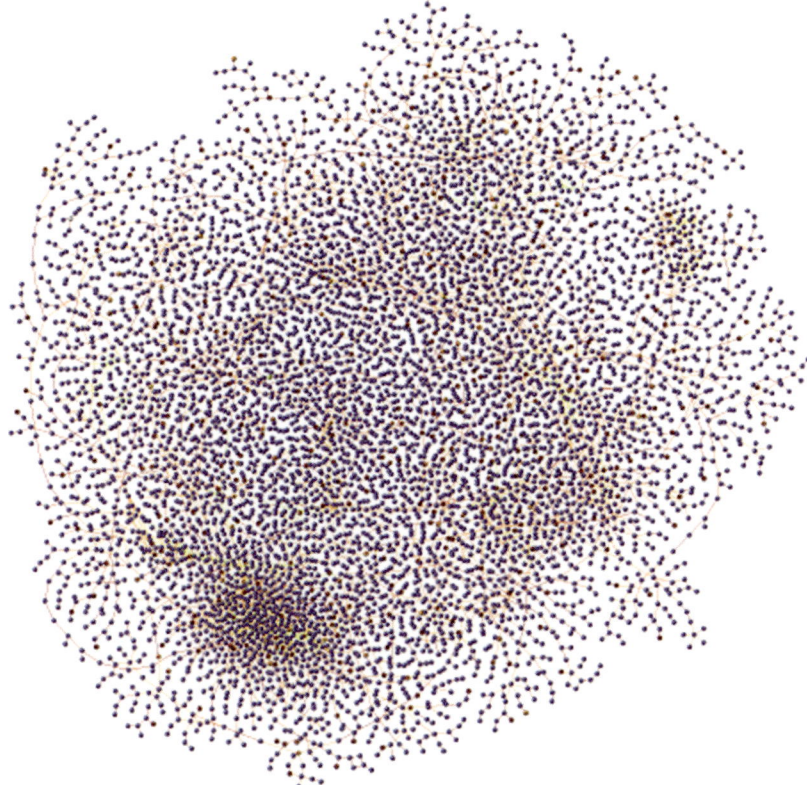

1-Ruth Mace, Clare J. Holden, and Stephen Shemman, *The Evolution of Cultural Diversity: A Phylogenetic Approach,* UCL Press, London (2005).

2-Sergi Valverde, Ricard V. Sole, Mark Bedau and Norman Packard, *Topology and Evolution of Technology Innovation Networks,* Physical Review E 76, 32767 (2007).

3-Luffiffis M. A. Bettencourt, David I. Kaiser, Jasleen Kaur, Carlos Castillo-Chavez, and David E. Wojick, *Population modeling of the emergence and development of scientific fields,* Scientometrics 75(3), 495-518 (2008).

FIG. 1- Graphic representation of the patent citation network for the rst 7000 patents in the USPTO database (http://www.uspto.gov), starting in 1963. Node and link color reflects the local density of connections. The network is quite heterogeneous, where a few patents are more heavily cited than the rest. In addition, patents appear to be clustered in the network according to the particular technological eld they belong to.

Canvi i Temps

Bestiario

Canvi (change) and *Temps (time)* are two navigation spaces within a network composed of articles, web pages, people and links related to the field of complexity science. This research, which is both historic (papers as far back as 1927 are reviewed) and crosscutting (containing more than 30 categories from different fields and disciplines), offers a broad overview of the foci, strategies, tactics, research methodologies and topics of interest that make up the field of complexity science. *Canvi* and *temps* offers two distinct ways to explore the content and their relationships in this field.

The primary structure of the database is a bipartition made up of content and tags. Existing relationships between contents and tags suggest new relationships. The networks emerging point towards interesting relationships and possible new connections among the contents.

Canvi (Change)

Canvi is a branch of a main axis of research into navigation interfaces in networks that Bestiario developed and dubbed. In essence, it is an interface which allows one to navigate through a network maintaining a constant local perspective around a node while moving about through means of the relationships. What is unique about *Canvi* is that it has pioneered new techniques for positioning the nodes and their relationships in space. In particular, *Canvi* combines a number of different techniques (geometric paradigms), smoothly alternating between them. In other words, the representation is constantly changing (breathing), and in this way offers a broader perspective of the structure of the local network. *Canvi* is a prototype that explores this technique extensively.

Temps (Time)

A desire to track changes over time in the topics of interest within complexity science (from 1927, the first time this term was used, through the present) emerged from conversations among members of the research group. *Temps* makes it possible to visualize the changes in the intensity of the use of tags over years.

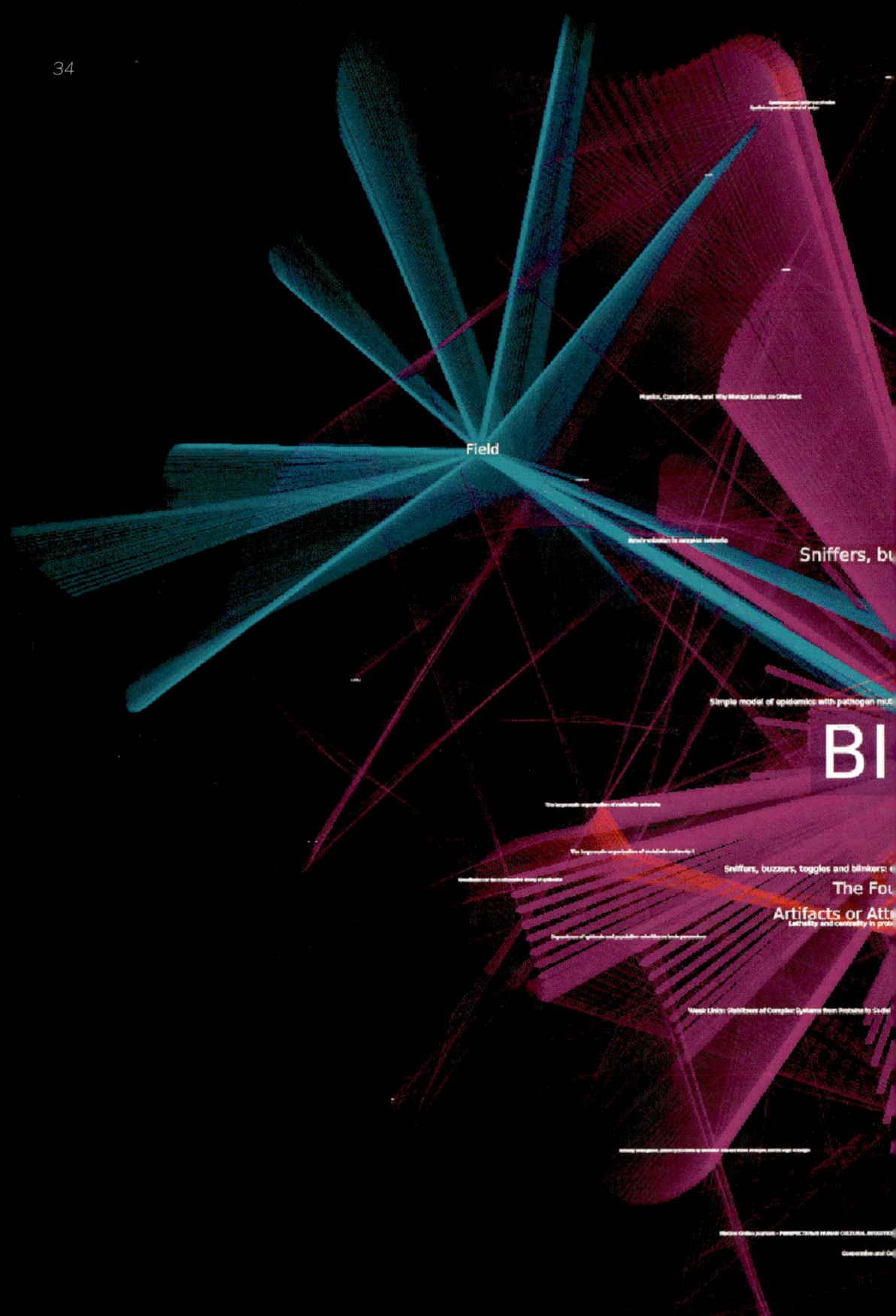

Field

Sniffers, bu

Mystics, Computation, and Why Biology Looks so Different

Synchronization in complex networks

Simple model of epidemics with pathogen mut

BI

The large-scale organization of metabolic networks

The large-scale organization of metabolic networks I

Sniffers, buzzers, toggles and blinkers: e

The Fou

Artifacts or Attr

Lethality and centrality in prot

Weak Links: Stabilizers of Complex Systems from Proteins to Social

ms of speciation and diversity

gles and blinkers: dynamics of regulatory and signaling pathways in the cell I
[FREE_PAPER]
he Role of Computation in Complex Regulatory Networks

Structure and Function of Complex Networks
The structure and function of complex networks
Neutral fitness landscapes in signalling networks

LOGY

Neutral fitness landscapes in signalling networks I

Population growth and collapse in a multiagent model of the Kayenta Anasazi in Long House Valley
sion of Life: Fractal Geometry and Allometric Scaling of Organisms
ects of Resolution on the Little Rock Lake Food Web

Autopoiesis and the origin of bacteria

A God of creativity

Degeneracy and complexity in biological systems

The Evolution of Cooperation

ON THE PERSPECTIVE OF THE ORIGIN OF SPECIES

Evolutionary self-organization in complex fluids

Extracts from a Skype conversation

Santiago Ortiz: I suppose that the challenges we face now are: to integrate content and records and to organize and enrich them. Beyond that, from my perspective, what remains is to carry out a project that would enable us to navigate through this information and its structure. What I hope is that, in addition to the project, the tasks of integrating and organizing might be useful and informative in and of themselves. I mean, as I mentioned to Irma, that the process be not only a means but an end.

Irma Vilà: Yes, I have mentioned that already...

Santiago Ortiz: One of the goals of this process, and one that must be strengthened in the project, is to get the records coming from different people to talk to each other. Part of the richness of this kind of integration is that contents will not be compartmentalized by their format or by the person who entered them.

Santiago Ortiz: To integrate all of this, we need a single repository of information, which will be an account on Delicious. This account should be thought of as a database because, in fact, it is, even though it doesn't store images or videos. If we save records of that type as files, in effect it will be essentially the same thing.

Santiago Ortiz: Going back to the issue of relationships, I had mentioned that the structure will be partitioned in two, tags and items (there will also be bundles, but for now let's focus on the two most essential elements) such that there will not be a priori relationships between items nor between tags. Instead there will be an "obvious" way to create relationships between items. Can any of you think of such a way?

Michele Catanzaro: "plan the bipartitioned web" :—) If two items have a common tag, they are co-related.

**Santiago Ortiz (Bestiario)
and Michele Catanzaro, Pere Monras,
Oriol Vallès,Carles Tardío & Irma Vilà**

Santiago Ortiz: Exactly, in this way an "interesting" network will form in which every node has some relationships.

Pere Monràs: not too dense and not too sparse

Santiago Ortiz: And, in this way it will be navigable, though not completely controllable. There will always be isolated nodes and nodes that are hyper-connected, a fundamental feature of "interesting" networks.

Pere Monràs: Yes, yes. There are papers that raise this issue as well.

Santiago Ortiz: In technical terms, we can ask ourselves if a network like this is "interesting", in other words, scalable. And the answer is "yes" bearing in mind that the threshold of relatedness will become more rigorous as the number of nodes increases. Scalable networks have many of the same properties that are suited for a network with low connectivity and sortability, although you can travel quickly from one node to another.

...

Irma Vilà: Great, then if you all agree, we can begin wrapping up. Do any of you have other comments, suggestions or outstanding questions?

Oriol Valles Codina: Basically, we'll have to clean up a little to standardize certain tags and retag bearing in mind what we have learned today.

Carles Tapi: I know, the more the better, but what would be the optimal number of bookmarks to ensure that the interface works well (in the order of...)?

Santiago Ortiz: Once we have surpassed 200, we'll have reached a good amount. Beyond this number, up to about 2000 would be perfect. In any case, whether we have 100 or 100.000.000 nodes, the essence of scalable networks is that you can still see everything clearly on the local scale.

Information Flow in an Organization through the Monitoring of Emails

Over the last decade we have witnessed the ever-increasing use of email as a vital tool of communication in our society. Its use in organizations is no exception to this trend, and a great deal of the internal information flow within a company takes place in this form, albeit supplemented by more "traditional" forms of communication such as personal meetings or phone calls, which are less easy to measure.

An organization's internal mail server can monitor the use of email and thus produce an X-ray of its "informal" structure, so called by contrast with the "formal" structure of the levels of hierarchy. We can then use this data to measure how far apart these two structures are.

The information stored by the server includes the identities of the sender and receiver of each message, but not the content. A first analysis based solely on the number of messages sent would allow us to determine whether the individual users and groups follow the predicted pattern in terms of information flow and communicate with the expected users or groups. The number of messages within each group should be balanced with the number of messages sent out to the exterior.

But if we want a more "global" view of our system, the best thing is to construct what we might call the *organization's email network*, by assigning each user a node in that network and recording a link between two users when a channel of communication is established, along with certain

Albert Díaz-Guilera & Àlex Arenas

additional requirements (that the communication be in both directions, that there be a minimum of messages, that possible sources of spam be eliminated, etc.).

Once the network has been constructed, its visualization will allow us to make a first qualitative analysis of the structure of the information flow. A network of how many hundreds of nodes can be visualized well using simple algorithms. Thus a larger network requires a mere display of complex algorithms, specifically developed for this purpose.

Recent methods developed by scientists in a variety of disciplines (from computer science to biology, by way of physics and mathematics) have laid the emphasis on what is known as the analysis of communities. Within many of the networks we analyse (biological, technological, social…) there are substructures which are more densely connected to each other than to the rest of the network, and these would be the *communities*. For example, it is easy to imagine common interest groups in a social network, as well as it is easy to imagine subnetworks in a technological network with geographical constraints. In particular, the analysis of communities in email networks allows better visualization in networks with more than a hundred nodes. And it is this end result that can be compared to the formal structure to give a measure of whether the organization is functioning as it should.

Relationship Mining

Undressing the social network: considering all e-mail interactions in an academic social network (right) yields to a highly dense and connected social network, while strong interactions (based on the individual relative frequency of communication) render the social group sparser and disconnected.

Each day trillions of emails, phone calls, comments on blogs, twitter messages, exchanges in online social networks are made. Not only the number of communications has increased, but also each of these transactions leaves a digital trace that can be recorded to reconstruct our high-frequency human activity. It is not only the amount and variety of data that is recorded what is important. Also its high-frequency character and its comprehensive nature have allowed researchers, companies and agencies to investigate individual and group dynamics at an unprecedented level of detail, and to apply them to client modeling, organizational analysis or epidemic spreading.[1]

However, wether for technical or privacy reasons, only the existence but not the content of those exchanges is known. Thus we can quantify the intensity and frequency of the interaction but not its type. For decades, social science has measured relationships between individuals in the currency of tie strength, introduced by Granovetter.[2] Weak ties (loose acquaintances) can help to disseminate ideas and/or innovations between different groups, to find a job or new information; while strong ties (family, trusted friends) hold together organizations and social groups and can affect emotional health. Despite its success to explain these phenomena, tie strength of human relationships is vaguely defined in most large-scale social empirical works. Specifically, relationships are generally quantified by the intensity or duration of communication, although they are known to have significant drawbacks as tie strength predictor.[3-4] Multiplexity, rhythm and depth of the communication seem to be better predictors of

Esteban Moro

tie strength than intensity.[4] Incorporating those metrics in the data mining of online communication might improve the definition of relationships between individuals and in turn transform our understanding of individual dynamics and its impact in our lives, organizations and society.[5] The challenge is to unveil social relationships in social media and not just mere interactions between individuals, which in general over–represent the real structure of a social group[6] (see figure). And this is of paramount importance to understand the propagation of ideas, opinions, commercial messages, in social networks, since most links declared in social networks might be meaningless from a relationship point of view.

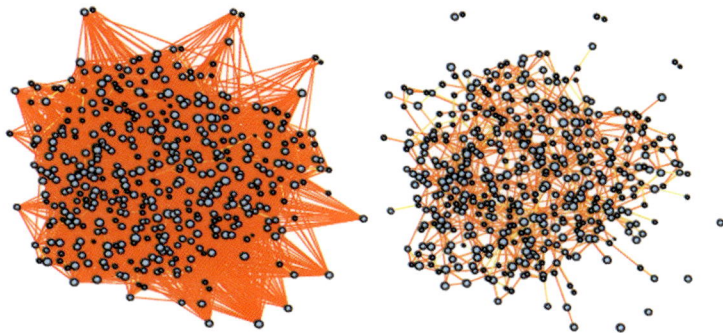

1-D. Lazer et al. *Computational Social Science*, Science 323, 721 (2009)

2-M. S. Granovetter, *The Strength of Weak Ties*, The American Journal of Sociology 78(6), 1360 (1973)

3-P. V. Marsden, and K. E. Campbell *Measuring Tie Strength* Social Forces 63(2), 482 (1990).

4-E. Gilbert and K. Karahalios, *Predicting Tie Strength* with Social Media, presented in CHI 2009.

5-C. T. Butts, *Revisting the Foundations of Network Analysis*, Science 325, 414 (2009)

6-B. A. Huberman, D. M. Romero, and F. Wu, *Social networks that matter*, First Monday 14(1) (2009)

The Parliament of Finance

In early 2004, Bruno Latour and Peter Weibel issued an unusual call for proposals for a very particular kind of show. An exhibition titled "Making Things Public" was to be held in 2005 at ZKM (Zentrum für Kunst und Medientechnologie) in Karlsruhe. The exhibition ought to be about representation, yes, but not only about "representation in the usual political sense (election, delegation, vote)" nor about representation exclusively considered "in the usual scientific sense (information, correspondence, truth)". The exhibition, collaborators were told, was about the sites "where various kinds of people meet the various kinds of things they have to talk about". Of course, screens of financial data flows had to sneak in. "The Parliament of Finance" (an installation created by Fabian Muniesa and Daniel Beunza) was a depiction of one critical event: the merger between computer industry giants Hewlett-Packard and Compaq. The merger, first announced on September 4th 2001, prompted great expectation and set off a lively debate until its final completion on May 3rd 2002. Many voices rose for and against the merger in a variety of manners: announcements, public campaigns, pressure on stock prices, votes, financial analysis, arbitrage models, private conversations, lawsuits, and so forth. The parliament of finance is manifold, but it was here presented as a collection of screen captures taken from a Bloomberg terminal, one similar to the thousands of screens that traders used in order to scrutinize the merger. Each screen capture was presented in the form of a framed color print, with an exhibition notice providing comments on such things as the nature of the topic or the expressiveness of the color composition. Captured in print, motionless, set away from the noise of trading rooms, these images invited to

Fabian Muniesa & Daniel Beunza

seize the market in a freeze frame. They also pointed out the very explicit style of expression that such data technologies have prompted in the material culture of financial life.[1] The very matter of finance is formed by these landscapes of data: data which are both quantitative and qualitative, data which stand both as what the market is and as what the market looks at.

1- See D. Beunza and F. Muniesa, 2005, "Listening to the spread plot", in B. Latour and P. Weibel, eds., *Making Things Public: Atmospheres of Democracy,* Cambridge (Massachusetts), MIT Press, pp. 628-633.

Models

Competition vs Cooperation in Complex Systems

People are, there can be no doubt, complex animals. We sometimes act on whims or impulses that we barely understand ourselves. We are, unlike the *Homo economicus* of traditional economic theory, prone to irrational behaviour. Given the same set of choices, different people make quite different decisions. What hope is there for capturing this psychological complexity in precise models of human behaviour that, acted out on a computer say, will generate anything like the group dynamics that we see in human populations?

Very little, you might think. But the past several decades have furnished many examples of models that produce startlingly realistic mass behaviour, based on 'rules' of human interaction and decision-making that look laughably, even insultingly crude. How can this be? Does it mean that our apparent free will is just an illusion?

Not exactly — but it implies that in many social situations that free will counts for rather little. What matters, it seems, is not *how* we make up our minds, but the mere fact that we do so through interactions with others, and in circumstances where our available options are highly constrained. Take road traffic: every driver is in one sense a free agent, and yet computer models that ascribe to individuals little more than the wish to drive at a preferred speed but a readiness to slow down to avoid collisions will generate all the kinds of complex flow patterns — phantom jams (which seem to have no "cause"), stop-and-go waves of congestion, synchronized motion — that are seen in reality.

Philip Ball

The field called statistical physics helps us to see why this is so. It is a science developed to understand the properties of inanimate matter when composed of many interacting entities: molecules of gas or liquid, say, or electrons moving through metals, or arrays of magnetic atoms or grains of sand undergoing avalanches and making dunes. One of the most striking findings of the field is that in such systems, often the details do not matter: the same types of behaviour and organization are seen in widely different physical systems. There are *universal* kinds of behaviour — and what's more, these are *collective* modes, arising from the mere fact of (rather than the precise nature of) the mutual influences of the component entities. Often the key factor may not be the exact "rules" of interaction, but the networks that these interactions create among the particles.

And this universality jumps the divide between the inanimate and animate worlds: similar patterns are found in colonies of bacteria or swarms of ants or fish. We should scarcely be surprised, then, that they reach also into the human social world: that our societies and institutions and movements too can sometimes resemble, in its average or statistical behaviour, a landslide or a glass or water freezing to ice. We are not *that* special. As the American writer Ralph Waldo Emerson put it, "The sublime laws play indifferently through atoms and galaxies."

Life
Writer

Laurent Mignonneau & Christa Sommerer

Life Writer is an old-fashioned typewriter that was transformed into a computer interface upon which users can interact using the normal functions of the machine. It stands on an old table with a projection from above oriented directly onto the paper. This creates the impression of the paper becoming the computer screen, since the movement of the typewriter's paper tray is seamlessly linked with the movement of the projected image.

When a user writes text on this typewriter, the text transforms into artificial life forms that appear on the paper of the typewriter as if directly emerging from the machine. These spider-like creatures run around frenetically trying to find text to eat. When the user types some more letters, the creatures will quickly snap it up, and once they have eaten enough text, they will reproduce and fill the whole surface of the paper. The user can also kill the creatures by pushing them off the paper or squeezing them back into the machine. The creatures are programmed with genetic algorithms, so they are semi-autonomous and follow their own internal rules of metabolization and reproduction. The whole process of writing text on *Life Writer* becomes a process of giving life to thoughts and having thoughts themselves evolve, escape and reconfigure. *Life Writer* is an extraordinary project, not only in the application of new technologies to sculptural form and in combining old and new technology through a media archaeological interface; it is also an example of an art form in which interactive art begins to evolve towards a "living art" in itself.

The creation and manipulation of fascinating visual images in an interactive environment where participants also engage in the act of creation raises fundamental questions about human interaction with increasingly "intelligent" machines and possible levels of human-machine symbiosis.

Life Writer is part of the collection of the ITAU Cultural Sao Paulo, Brazil. Originally developed in 2006 for the "All Digital" show at the MOCA Museum of Contemporary Art in Cleveland, curated by Margo Crutchfield.

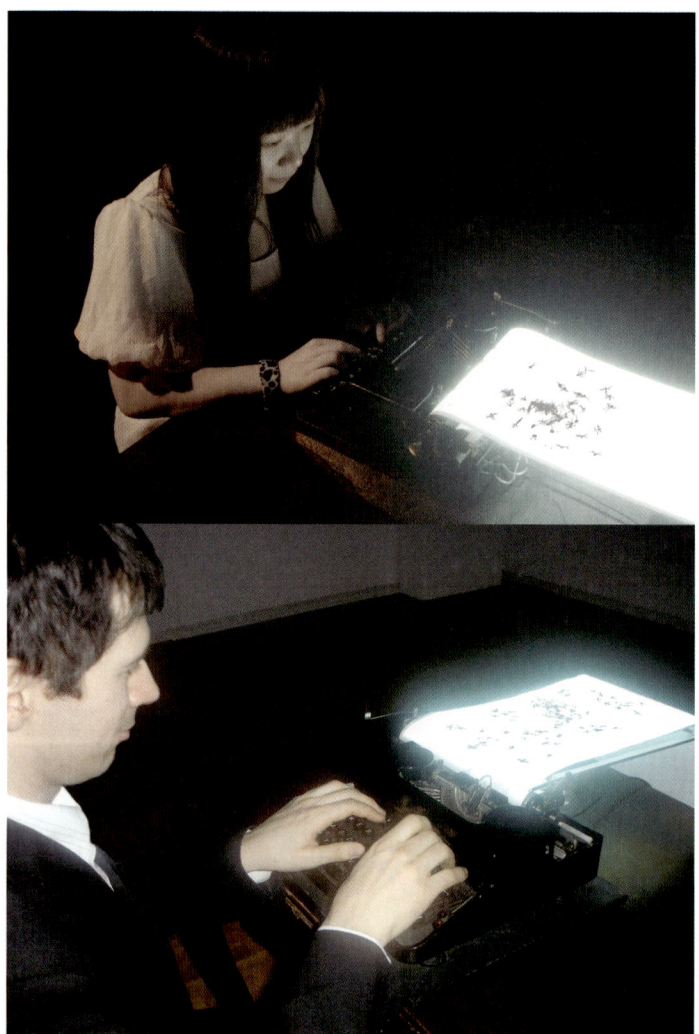

Life Writer © 2006, Laurent Mignonneau & Christa Sommerer

Econophysics

Almost every physicist by now has heard of the fast-growing subdiscipline of "econophysics", a field characterized by collaborations between physicists and economists and focused on asking if new insights or even laws could emerge if the concepts and approaches of statistical physics were brought to bear on questions that originate in economics.

And almost everyone, physicist or nonphysicist, has by now heard that the economies of every country — large or small, Eastern or Western — are witnessing truly huge fluctuations. So it is natural to ask "Does econophysics have anything to say about the current financial/economic turmoil?"

The answer to this question is a resounding "Yes!" since econophysics is statistical physics applied to the economy, and fluctuations are the substance of statistical physics. In economics, the probability density function (pdf) of price changes has been studied for over 100 years, ever since the Ph.D. thesis of Bachelier in 1900 analyzed real data — without benefit of computers. Then, to understand the pattern he witnessed, he introduced a model which today we call the drunkard's walk. This is the model immortalized to the general public in the aphorism "random walk down Wall Street."

Approximately 50 years ago, as more data became available, it became clear that the drunkard's walk fails to describe all the data. The term "fat tail" was used to describe the mathematical counterpart of this statement, that the pdf of price changes contains many more events in

H. Eugene Stanley

the tail than predicted by the Gaussian pdf characterizing the drunkard's walk. Nonetheless, more than 99 percent of the then available data were reasonably approximated by a Gaussian, so a terminology grew up where events corresponding to these fat tails became known as "rare events" or sometimes called "tsunamis." Since there was no theory for them, some argued, and since they are indeed very rare, we can as well ignore them. The word "outlier" is sometimes used to describe a data point that does not conform to the widely used Gaussian distribution of price fluctuations.

Then along came the physicists, starting about 15 years ago when the neologism "econophysics" was coined by this author to describe efforts to apply physics approaches to this and other questions of interest in economics. This field can trace its roots to Newton and Copernicus, two physicists who worked extensively on economics problems, and to a number of others over the centuries who applied to economics the fundamental approach of physics. Firstly, to be eternally skeptical of everything — especially in this case of the practice of calling something that does not agree with a theory an "outlier" or "tsunami".

And, perhaps most importantly, to collect as many data as possible before making any theory to interpret them.

Unlike traditional topics in physics, where collecting data often requires imagination and sometimes years of painstaking labor, in the case of price changes every transaction of every stock is recorded and stored. Apparently all the data were not analyzed, so two Boston University graduate students, Paramaswaram Gopikrishnan and Vasiliki Plerou (now happily married!), set about to acquire and analyze the data on every transaction...such a voluminous data set that their University computer system were required to acquire a significant addition to its storage capacity.

When they analyzed these data — 200 million of them — in exactly the same fashion that Bachelier had analyzed data almost a century earlier, they made a startling discovery. The pdf of price changes was not Gaussian plus outliers, as previously believed. Rather, all the data — including data previously termed outliers — conformed to a single pdf encompassing both everyday fluctuations and "once in a century" fluctuations. Instead of a Gaussian or some correction to a Gaussian, they found a power law pdf with exponent -4, a sufficiently large exponent that the difference from a Gaussian is not huge, the probability of a "once in a century" event of, say, 100 standard deviations is $exp^{(-10,000)}$ ~approx $10^{(-347)}$ for the Gaussian, but simply $10^{(-8)}$ for an inverse quartic law. If one analyzes a data set containing 200 million data in two years, this means there are only two such events — in two years!

Now which is better, the concept of "everyday fluctuations" which can be understood/modeled with a drunkard's walk, complemented by a few "once in a century" outliers. Or a single empirical law with no outliers but for which a complete theory does not exist despite promising progress by Xavier Gabaix of NYU's Stern School of Management and his collaborators? Here we come to one of the most salient differences between traditional economics and the econophysicists: economists are hesitant to put much stock in laws that have no coherent and complete theory supporting them, while physicists cannot afford this reluctance. Many of our "laws" have proved useful long before any theoretical underpinning was developed...Newton's laws and Coulomb's law to name but two.

And all of us are loathe to accept even a well-documented empirical law that seems to go against our own everyday experience. For stock price fluctuations, we all experience calm periods of everyday fluctuations, punctuated by highly volatile periods that seem to cluster. So we would expect the pdf of stock price fluctuations to be bimodal, with a broad maximum centered around, say, 1-3 standard deviations and then a narrow peak centered around, say, 50 standard deviations. And it is easy to show that if we do not have access to "all the data" but instead sample only a small fraction of the 200 million data recently analyzed, then this everyday experience is perfectly correct, since the rare events are indeed rare and we barely recall those that are "large but not that large."

The same is true for earthquakes: our everyday experience teaches us that small quakes are going on all the time but are barely noticeable except by those who work at seismic detection stations. And every so often occurs a "once in a century" truly horrific event, such as the famous San Francisco earthquake. Yet when seismic stations analyze all the data, they find not the bimodal distribution of everyday experience but rather a power law, the Gutenberg-Richter law, describing the number of earthquakes of a given magnitude.

Do we ignore the inverse quartic law that fits all the data but once-in-a-century events? Or do we design a financial system that has safeguards to minimize the damage when one of these rare events actually occurs?

Luci.
With No Name
and No Memory

José Manuel Berenguer

Nature, irrespective of the organization of the type of material in question, is full of oscillators. From emissions of energy in the form of radiation, each with its characteristic frequency, to pulsars and the planets orbiting around the stars, geological systems such as temperature throughout the Earth's history, stock-market systems, prices, everything can be seen in terms of oscillating systems. The homeostatic mechanisms of animals, the thousands of cellular genes that regulate each other in the genome expression system, the networks of cells and molecular that determine immune response, the cells of the Bundle of Hiss which regulate the heartbeat, the billions of neurons in the neural networks that are the material basis of mental activity, learning and, ultimately, thought, are all instances of systems with a capacity for self-organization.

Self-organization also occurs in firefly colonies. A male firefly sends out a flashing signal to which a female will respond if she finds the pattern of intermittence sufficiently sexy. In some colonies, the frequencies of light emissions tend to converge with one another and, in time, to match perfectly. Here we have a fascinating biological oscillator, capable of producing by itself an endless number of aesthetic experiences: whole ponds, trees, mangroves, inhabited by huge colonies of these insects end up emitting periodic flashes of green light in the jungle night. Each insect's independent oscillators, after a process of adaptation in which the colony as a whole produces a certain number of chaotic pulsation patterns determined by each firefly's independent pulsation frequency join together in a single rhythmic flashing. They synchronize.

Fascinated by this vision, I wanted to mimic the emergent behaviour of firefly colonies electronically in an installation. The first model I made, in 1994, had five electronic fireflies. The installation now has 21 electronic elements and 128 computational elements. When the ambient light is strong, each electronic object pulses independently in its own rhythm. When the time amount of light falls below a certain level, when the infrared signals can be picked received by the neighbouring receivers, the system tends to stabilize and large areas are created in which the objects gradually come to pulse in synchrony. The computational elements, which individually have no name or memory, mimic that behaviour and project it into the space occupied by the electronic elements. From the individual behaviour of the latter, Luci is simply an unexpected emergence and a member of a class of entities that take me back once again to the questions that have almost obsessively haunted my mind since I first heard Luigi Nono pose them to a group of young composers who couldn't see what all this could have to do with music. Is there really anything entirely continuous in this world? In the realm of matter and energy, of course, the answer is no, but in the mind can discontinuity generate genuine continuity? Some people think that the Continuum Hypothesis will some day be proved false, and in fact it is the fundamental paradigm of traditional writing and also of the art that uses discrete machines such as computers. What is the true meaning of representing and simulating discreetly what manifests itself to human perception as an instance of continuity? I have the feeling that the answer is not in matter or in signals. It seems to me, rather, to be related in some way to the imaginaries of our understanding.

Problems of Social Consensus: Voting, Language, Culture...

The issue of social consensus is currently being addressed from general concepts and methods used to understand collective phenomena in Statistical and Nonlinear Physics: The problem is to determine when and how the dynamics of a set of interacting agents that can choose among several options leads to a consensus in one of these options, or when a state with several coexisting options prevails. Examples include opinion dynamics and political vote, language competition (death or coexistence of languages) and cultural dissemination (globalization-polarization transitions). The answer to these questions depends on the two basic ingredients characterizing interactions among the agents: 1) the mechanism of agentagent interaction, 2) who interacts with whom (the social network). Current models implement separately different mechanisms with the aim of establishing cause-effect relations. Some of these mechanisms are random imitation, following local majorities, homophily or strengthening of similarities, individual thresholds against social pressure, etc. Social networks considered come either from real data (for example data on mobile phone or email interactions) or from current theories of complex networks, including networks with long range links (small world), networks with hubs (scale free) or networks with well characterized community structures.

A pedagogical example is the one of interaction by random imitation of agents with two options. Reaching consensus in one of the two options for large social groups crucially depends on the network topology. An important counterintuitive result is that long range links (interactions among distant agents) do not promote reaching consensus, but lead to a dynamical coexistence in which agents keep changing their option. Such long range interactions typically exist in our global society (internet) as opposed to traditional local village interactions.

Maxi Sanmiguel

Following pioneering work by the political scientist Robert Axelrod, problems of cultural dynamics have been analyzed in some detail for the perspective of statistical physicists. The question addressed by Axelrod was: "if people tend to become more alike in their beliefs, attitudes and behavior when they interact, why do not all differences eventually disappear?" He proposed a model to explore competition between globalization and the persistence of cultural diversity. Culture is defined as a set of individual attributes subject to social influence. The model implements a mechanism of homophilic interactions and illustrates how an interaction mechanism of local convergence can generate global polarization (persistence of cultural diversity).

However, culturally polarized states have been shown to be unstable against phenomena of cultural drift in a fixed social network. Persistence of cultural diversity can be understood as a consequence of co-evolving dynamics of agents and network: The social network evolves in tandem with the collective action it makes possible (Circumstance makes men as much as men make circumstances or Cultures of change/Changing cultures). Concerning the effect of mass media in the processes of cultural globalization two important claims follow from these studies: 1) Perhaps surprisingly, a strong mass media message leads to social polarization, but mass media is efficient in producing cultural homogeneity in conditions of weak (and local) broadcast of a message (the power of being subtle).2) The role of the social network.

Social interactions can lead to a social consensus in a direction different from the one broadcasted by mass media provided that there are long range links in the network of interactions. Long range links make possible that collective self organization defeats external messages.

Embodied Language Games

Luc Steels, Michael Spranger & Martin Loetzsch

The installation shows a series of experiments to see under what circumstances and by what mechanisms physical humanoid robots could self-organize a symbolic communication system without human intervention. This challenge raises tremendously difficult problems because we need to understand and artificially simulate visual perception, conceptualisation of reality for language, interaction scripts, and language processing. We need to understand not only how robots can learn concepts and language

from others but also how they can extend their existing language system with new words or constructions to express new concepts and talk about situations they have never encountered. Then we need to orchestrate the coordination between the languages and concepts that each robot constructs so that a coherent shared language effectively emerges.

The first experiments[1] focus on body language. Robots first develop a self-model by executing random movements before a mirror so that they can learn the relation between their internal sensori-motor experiences (based on signals sent to the actuators, proprioceptive signals sensing the movements of the body) and the visual experiences they get from the mirror. Next they play language games where one robot asks another one to do a certain action and the game is a success if the other one executes the requested action. At the start of the experiments robots do not share concepts nor words for describing actions but our experiments have shown that they can nevertheless progressively self-organise a successful communication system for body language.

The second experiments shown[2] focus on spatial language. Now the robots play a game in which they draw the attention to objects in their environment using the spatial positions of these objects. For example, they might say something equivalent to "the block to my left." Here again robots start without a prior ontology of spatial concepts and without a language expressing them. But by playing the game, and doing the right adaptations of their internal memory states, the robots progressively achieve communicative success.

1-Steels, L. and M. Spranger (2008) The Robot in the Mirror. Connection Science, 20(4):337-358.
1-Steels, L. and M. Spranger (2008) Can body language shape body image? In: Proceedings of Artificial Life XI. The MIT Press, Cambridge Ma. pp. 577-584.

2-Steels, L. and M. Loetzsch (2009) Perspective Alignment in Spatial Language. In: Coventry, K., J. Bateman and T. Tenbrink (2009) Spatial Language in Dialogue. Oxford University Press, Oxford.
2-Steels, L. and M. Spranger (2009) How experience of the body shapes language about space. IJCAI-09. Pasadena, Ca. AAAI Press.

2-Steels, L. (1995) A self-organizing spatial vocabulary. Artificial Life Journal, 2(3): 319-332.

Self-organization of Social Systems

The Importance of Local Interactions for Social Cooperation

Social systems work in a wonderful way. They are largely based on self-organization. Social norms, for example, influence and guide our behavior thousands of times every day and thereby determine the way in which we interact with each other. By prescribing certain "roles", they are setting standards of how we ought to behave in certain situations. While this narrows down our freedom of decision-making to a certain degree, often we are happily contributing to the system of norms, as it simplifies our lives: It reduces uncertainty, bargaining efforts, and conflicts, and thereby it makes our everyday interactions smoother and more successful.

Yet, it is largely unknown how these social forces are created, and how social self-organization leads to the emergence of norms and social order. The problem seems related to the establishment of cooperation among people. Cooperation is natural in win-win situations, but what will happen in social dilemmas? If people have to contribute to a public good (a clean environment, a social benefit system, etc.) or if they are sharing a public good (like natural resources, road capacity, etc.), a "tragedy of the commons" will often result. That is, people will tend to make insufficient contributions to the public good, and they will overuse it. We are now facing this dilemma on a global scale, as mankind has to solve the global warming problem, which is expected to have serious impact on earth's climate, the ecosystem, land use, food production, and water availability. Large-scale migration, conflicts, and social instabilities will be likely consequences.

Dirk Helbing

Although the problem of managing the commons is well known from everyday life, humans behave more cooperatively than economists would have expected. Scientists from various fields are therefore trying to reveal the hidden secrets of cooperation. In fact, there are many mechanisms which can support the establishment of cooperation. Among them, genetic relatedness, repeated interactions, reputation effects, the formation of friendship networks, the competition between groups, or the punishment of non-cooperative behaviors, to mention only a couple of them. It has also been found that local interactions can support the survival of cooperative behavior, but the birth and spreading of cooperation in a "nasty" world, where everybody cheats everybody else in the beginning, appears to be quite unlikely.

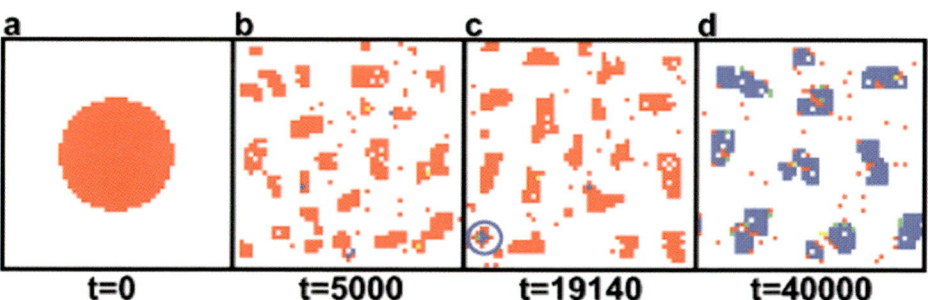

a   b   c   d

t=0   t=5000   t=19140   t=40000

FIG 1: Illustration of the birth and spreading of cooperation through local interactions among mobile, success-oriented individuals (red = cheaters/free-riders, blue = co-operators) [from: D. Helbing and W. Yu, PNAS 106, 3680-3685 (2009)].

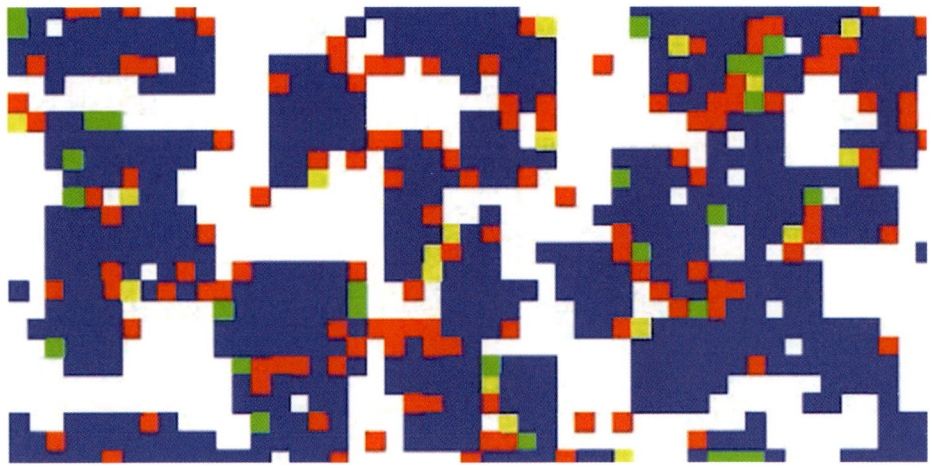

FIG 2: shows snapshots of a computer simulation, where cooperative individuals are represented by blue squares and free-riders by red ones. The simulation starts with a nasty world, where everyone is cheating, but after some time, a cooperative cluster is born, and cooperation eventually spreads all over the world. In conclusion, there is hope that humankind may eventually be able to come up with collective action against climate change and other problems. Nevertheless one must be aware that global interactions can seriously weaken the social forces that support cooperation (see Figure 3).

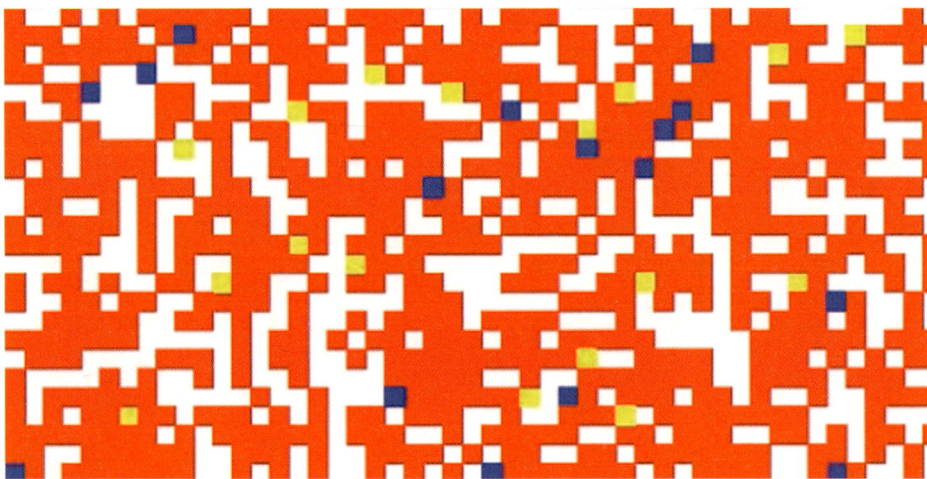

FIG 3: Establishment of cooperation in a world with local interactions and local migration (left) in comparison with the breakdown of cooperation in a world with global interactions and global migration (right). (red = cheaters/free-riders, blue = cooperators) [after: D. Helbing, W. Yu, and H. Rauhut, submitted to Journal of Mathematical Sociology (2009)].

However, it turns out that a social system can turn from hell to heaven (i.e. from a battle of everybody against everyone else to a cooperative world). This can happen, if the following effects come together: 1) Individuals copy the behavior of more successful neighbors or friends. 2) Individuals move to other places (in geographical or social space), when they are not satisfied with their social environment. 3) Individuals check out new behavioral strategies or places from time to time. The third effect creates small clusters of cooperators sometimes, just by random coincidence. The second effect causes people to avoid unfriendly environments, and the first effects lets people imitate the behavior of more successful individuals, who belong to clusters of cooperators. Altogether, this leads to a segregation of cooperative people from non-cooperative ones (the "free-riders" or "cheaters"). Moreover, cooperative social environments reinforce cooperative behavior, which maintains cooperation over a long time.

POEtic-Cubes

Raquel Paricio
& Juan Manuel Moreno Aróstegui

Attention, Adaptation, Emergent Systems, Bio-inspiration and Artificial Life

"Attention is in some degree consciousness itself when it awakens."
Maria Zambrano

Attention has become a serious problem that has distracted and alienated the contemporary subject. Writers such as Walter Benjamin, Michel Foucault and Jonathan Crary clearly describe the disintegration that has created social exchanges in which the mechanical prevails over any conscious perception or rational attention. The project *POEtic-cubes* offers us an environment in which, starting from the basis of our sensation of movement and expanding this to take in the whole, we can arrive at a level of focused awareness that allows us to perceive the potential of a wider attention, an attention that facilitates a state of conscious presence. This is because the sculptural environment continually adapts and responds to the user's movements, thus configuring a space in constant change and mutation.

In realizing this work, an essential part of the process involved looking at how the experience of this phenomenon has been dealt with in Eastern culture, which historically has created many areas and activities where the phenomenon of attention was the base. Thus, activities such as the martial arts or the tea ceremony, over and above the immediate military or aesthetic objective, are intended to achieve a state of attention. *POEtic-cubes* is thus formalized as a space of attention to the body, to the space it occupies in the environment, to its movement and its relationship in emerging and adaptive environments, where no element acts in isolation but is part of a network, an emergence, a whole.

The installation

POEtic-cubes is a physical installation, a sculptural group that is organized and takes form in relation to the stimuli coming from the environment. The installation consists of nine cubes or autonomous robots which have been provided with some of the properties of a cell, so that we also refer to them as "cells". They can thus develop certain characteristics of living things and create a sculpture that is adapted to its environment. Their behaviour is centred on detecting and surrounding any human being who enters the space. The robots always maintain a distance from one another and from the centre of gravity of the users. They can be set in motion by a simple movement of the arm, which without arriving at actual tactile interaction, moves the whole sculptural group. In other words, any physical gesture made by of the user beyond his or her centre of gravity is detected by the group of robots and results in a synchrony of movement between users and robots. Whether the interaction involves one person or several cooperating with one another, the ability to manage the entire sculptural group at once, as if dancing with the robots, requires a high level of attention, maintaining which allows the users to obtain an expanded awareness of their relationship with their environment.

The sculptural group replicates the evolutionary process of a living being and undergoes a "cellular" change as a result of the interaction with the user.

The interaction

The cubes move in response to any body movement oriented towards their thermal sensors of this, without any tactile pressure being exerted on the robot. When the user tries to interact with a single robot they become aware that their actions are part of a network of nine interrelated robots. They can also interact with the whole group of robots, as if juggling nine objects at once, and try to make them form a luminous circle.

The behaviour

The sculpture appears in its initial state as a single cell, formed by the set of nine cubes, and then commences a process of division or mitosis when it detects that a user is present. Each of the cells that separates from the initial unit retains the same genetic structure as the stem cell, and this is represented by the colour of each robot's light, which is the same as the stem cell's. The colour then changes in saturation and intensity according to the distance between the robots and between robots and users. The sculptural group functions with emergent behaviour: in other words, all of the robots relate to one another in order to maintain an organized cooperative structure in space. Each robot knows its position and changes this in relation to the movements of the user, whom it attempts to surround at all times. If a robot were missing it would not destabilize the final figure, because the remaining robots would simply adjust their relative positions and distances. When a robot detects that its battery is low, it automatically stops the performance and sends all the robots to recharge independently, resuming the performance once the energy level is restored.

The use of bio-inspiration in *POEtic-cubes*

The special hardware was designed for the behaviour of the installation makes it possible to calculate in real time the position of each robot and the relations between robots and the user. The model is based on the previously developed bio-inspired hardware POEtic Tissue.[1]

The bio-inspired features of the installation are:

Phylogenesis (P): Each cell (cube) contains a copy of the configuration of the organism as a whole

Ontogenesis (O): The development of an organism out of the individual cells that constitute it.

Emergence (E): This is a distributed, local and completely autonomous system. The ultimately resulting organism — the form continually adopted by the nine cubes — is the product of the local interactions between its cells (cubes). This represents a significant difference from classic systems based on central control, in which each robot, instead of having an 'intelligence' with which to regulate its actions with respect to its neighbours, is simply directed to a certain position by the controller.

For more information about the project: http://www.evolvable.net/poetic

1-The main aim of the POEtic Tissue project is the development of a flexible electronic substrate (electronic tissue or chip) that can be implanted with some of the features found in living beings: evolution, development, self-replication and learning. Its use in society will be to resolve conflicts that require an immediate adaptive response. Research led by J. M. Aróstegui Moreno (UPC) and developed in five European universities. http://www.poetictissue.org

Is Chance Unique?
The Debate between Intrinsic and Accidental Randomness

The introduction of probability — and its closed relative: statistics — into social and economic sciences begun at the end of the Eighteenth century and developed through the Nineteenth century with names such as Vilfredo Pareto and Karl Pearson among many others. In physical sciences the appearance of these methods, associated with the establishment of kinetic theory and statistical mechanics, had a parallel and almost contemporary progress. Major names were: James C. Maxwell, Ludwig Boltzmann and Josiah W. Gibbs.

Both approaches tried to find regularities, and subsequently laws, in the seemingly lawless world of chance, luck and randomness, either in the inanimate world or in human activities. For the ancients chance was the manifestation of the will of gods and goddesses. Since, as often happened, gods' whims were unknown and unpredictable, hence chance, randomness and luck emerged. Curiously enough this primitive conception is in fact behind the classical view of chance which stemmed from Laplace: Chance is lack of knowledge — not of gods' wishes but from an incomplete knowledge of data. If a being (of course a supranatural one) knew, at a given initial instant, the positions and velocities of all particles of the universe, then he would undoubtedly find the state of the universe at any later time owing to the equations of classical mechanics. It is as if in throwing a coin, one knows the exact force exerted on the coin in magnitude and direction, the exact height from which it is thrown, as well as air velocity, elastic properties of the ground, and so on, then one would forecast with certainty, solving Newton equations of motion, whether it lands on head or tail.

This is the notion of chance in classical physics and it was the only concept of it for more than two centuries. However, during the first thirty years of the Twentieth century, a new field of knowledge was developed: quantum mechanics. After some vacillating beginnings oriented to find an explanation for the energy distribution of the black-body radiation — an ac-

Jaume Masoliver

---

count that classical physics failed to produce — by the end of the twenties of Nineteenth century, quantum mechanics had become a full-fledged theory of atomic physics. Major theoretical players were: M. Planck, A. Einstein, N. Bohr, L. de Broglie, M. Born, W. Heisenberg, P. Dirac and E. Schrödinger. In quantum mechanics, chance is an essential constituent of the theory, but it turns out to be of a different nature than that of classical thought. For the latter chance is accidental, arising from extrinsic causes.

In classical reasoning the notion of probability — the quantitative measure of chance — is a mathematical objectivization of the human deficiency of a complete and exact knowledge and ultimately a creation of the human mind, or as Siponoza expressed it: "It is only through the imagination that we look upon things as contingent [i.e., random] with reference to both the past and the future", and also: "It is the nature of reason to consider things not as contingent but as necessary."[1]

Yet quantum mechanics views probability not as a mathematical fiction but something endowed with physical reality. Therefore, to quantum mechanics chance is an intrinsic quality of nature and not merely an accident due to incomplete knowledge. This meant a severe blow on classical reasoning, for it introduced the lack of causality as an innate quality, specially in the atomic and subatomic domains. If we imagine a "microscopic coin" of atomic or molecular dimensions, one would be unable to forecast the result of trowing it even after knowing all necessary data, because, contrary to macroscopic (classical) physics, the laws governing the microscopic (quantum) dynamics imply an intrinsic randomness in the evolution of the system. It is often erroneously claimed that, ironically as it sounds, Einstein, i.e. the most prominent advocate of causality in physics and the philosopher who rejected the "dice-playing God", was the first to introduce the modern quantum-theoretic notion of probability, not as an expression of 75 insufficient knowledge of fine-scale parameters, as conceived in kinetic theory — and, by extension, in classical physics on the whole — but as an affirmation in a fundamental manner of chance as a single event.[2] In fact, the emergence of nonclassical reasoning was not confined to theoretical physics and had some philosophical background in some figures of the late Nineteenth century philosophy. We will cite Charles Sanders Pierce who contended, as early as 1868, that "nature is not regular" and that 'chance is a factor in the universe', he went even further by affirming the impossibility of the exact determination of any quantity, thus almost anticipating Heisenberg uncertainty principle.[3]

   Among physicists and philosophers alike the debate on the two kinds of randomness — that is, whether chance is intrinsic or accidental — has been going on and off since the late twenties of Nineteenth century. The controversy has often taken the form of heating discussions on causality versus indeterminism. Quantum advocates sustain that nature is fundamentally random while others, following the footsteps of Einstein, Schrödinger and de Broglie,[4] while granting quantum mechanics its impressive achievements, maintain that classical thought must not be ruled out, for there could be hidden variables whose lack of knowledge might result in an apparently intrinsic randomness. However, to mainstream physicists as long as quantum mechanics works — and it does so far — one should not bother about the strange philosophical implications of intrinsic chance.

   This note begun by stating the parallel development of the classical concept of probability in social and economic sciences on one hand, and physical sciences on the other. One may but wonder whether the debate on the nature of chance might be extended to social and economic sciences as well. In this regard some questions arise at once: does it have any sense to distinguish between intrinsic and accidental randomness as far as human behavior is concerned? Is there any empirical fact that supports such a distinction, as there was in physics? That is to say, is there a possible inherent randomness in human conduct? These are indeed thorny issues since — besides the great difficulty in obtaining reliable empirical observations on these matters — they affect delicate notions such as free will and the perception of reality. Be as it may, this is a far-reaching and most fundamental discussion which will have a long life well inside the twentyfirst century.

1-Quoted in Max Jammer's: *The Conceptual Development of Quantum Mechanics* (McGraw-Hill, New York, 1966), p. 286.

2-This is a widespread opinion even though Einstein never believed in any kind of essential randomness. See *Einstein, Philosopher-Scientist*, edited by P. A. Schilpp (The Library of Living Philosophers, Evanston, Ill. Second edition, 1951).

3-Other philosophers following similar lines of reasoning were: A. Cournot, C. Renouvier, E. Boutroux, S. Kierkegaardand H. Høffding, the latter is believed to have been influential on Niels Bohr's thought. See Max Jammer, op. cit. pp. 166-180.

4-Contrary to the orthodox interpretation of quantum mechanics, these scientists believed in an objective reality independent of the observer. For further discusssions on physics and reality see, for instance, Bernard d'Espagnat: *In Search of Reality* (Springer-Verlag, Berlin, 1983).

Humanism

From One to Multiplicity

It was a decisive event when the mathematician Riemann uprooted the multiple from its predicate state and made it a noun, 'multiplicity'. It marked the end of dialectics and the beginning of a typology and topology of multiplicities.
Gilles Deleuze and Felix Guattari, A Thousand Plateaus, 1988.

The beginning of a topology of multiplicities is linked here to changes in the capacities of numbers. In mathematics, numbers participate both in processes of ordering and in representing that order as value, says the anthropologist Helen Verran. The numerical process of ordering involves their use as ordinals, and typically involves a form of generalization where parts are derived from a whole, while the second — cardinal — dimension of number involves a use in which value is produced by engaging a specific one-to-many relation. This dual arithmetical role of number — in ordering and valuing — is conflated in Euclidean geometry, in which both order and value are given by the relation afforded by a fixed measure, a metric, or unit of magnitude, that was held to apply independently of any particular situation. In such uses, numbers are able to function as unremarkable but powerful indices, external markers of order and value in "one."

In the topological thinking of multiplicity, however, ordering and valuing are brought together without reference to an external measure, but rather by — or in — relations in which the performative capacities of number to order and value are locally combined in different ways to produce spaces more general than those described by Euclid. Indeed, a consequence of adopting multiple relations as their own measure is that the resulting space is manifold; it may be of n-dimensions. In the case of a fractal, in which the relation between part and whole is that of self-similarity, the space may be, for example, between one and two dimensions — a line becoming a plane. To put it another way, in topological mathematics 4 is not simply 2 x 2 or 2 + 2 (or 1 + 1 + 1 + 1), since the parts that comprise the whole (in relations of multiplicity) are always more than the elements in which it consists. In the evocative phrase adopted by Alain Badiou, there is an excess of inclusion over belonging.

Celia Lury

The event of multiplicity followed the recognition that when faced with the question of what number does and how it functions in the making of order and value, there were many exceptions. Of course, Riemann was not the only one to recognise these problems. Herman von Helmholtz observed, adding one raindrop to another does not make two, while Henri Lebesgue similarly noted that if you put a lion and a rabbit in a cage you do not usually end up with two animals. What is important about Helmholtz, Riemann and Lesbegues among others however is that they contributed to an interlinked set of developments in mathematics which enabled the analysis of what might happen if you put a lion and a rabbit in a cage. That is, to give another example, the development of topological mathematics has provided tools by which to analyse how it is that if you halve a litre of water at 100 degrees, you do not halve its temperature. In other words, it makes it possible to explore the dynamic properties of mathematical and other objects that remain invariant in Euclidean space. There is no external or unitary space of measurement in such topological analysis, instead space is analysed *substantially* through variability in, for example, temperature.

In modern topological mathematics then, numbers no longer just describe but increasingly construct and take on virtual properties, building generalised spaces of calculation. The use of such spaces — for calculation, observation and intervention — is increasingly common in, for example, the experimental processes of architecture, biology, economics and physics, but it is not confined to computer simulation. In the move from the one to multiplicity, both in and out of the screen, space is no longer experienced as a residuum, the inert context in which objects are produced and exchanged. Rather topological space is conceived as a medium of production, a surface of becoming or being-in. This space is not static but always in flux, and being-in or becoming is the (topological) spacing in which difference manifests and is constituted via other differentials. How to inhabit this space of becoming — how to engage the multiple — is a fundamental question today. If the very first notion of space was a solution to the problem of change, then topological space is fundamental to cultures of change now.

News Telescope

Prospect and Innovation Studio:
Terry Rosenberg, Mike Waller, Pete Rogers, Andrew Weatherhead,
Duncan Fairfax. Goldsmiths, University of London

The "News Telescope" is one of a number of prototypes of the "Mediating Place" research project (which is housed in the Leverhulme sponsored Spaces of Media Research Program, at Goldsmiths and undertaken by members of the Prospect and Innovation Studio).

"Mediating Place", is focused on an exploration of the ways in which various "locational" or 'locative' media — which are becoming an increasingly pervasive presence in our everyday lives — affect the way we relate to our world, or worlds, now and in the future. It is apparent that our environment (particularly urban) is increasingly mediatised — infused with media technologies and their concomitant content, therefore the project is also concerned with how this "media-full" environment, re-mediates our relationships to those objects and spaces to which we are connected, and, ultimately our relationships to each other as well. The project pays heed to the way we "place" the "media-things" that make-up our environment and also in how in these placements we make the spaces in which we carry out our lives significant — make the spaces of everyday practices into places that are meaningful to us.

We have designed media-things that present new arrangements and produce opportunities for new performances of media.

The media-things that we are designing are "propositional objects"; props to help understand future opportunities (proposals) of the new "performance" spaces of media and the technologies that produce them. The prop(osition)s are designed to act, in a sense, as an "apparatus criticus" looking critically and signalling "choices to be made" in future developments of media and its places (critical speculation). In so doing, they also act as critical "reflection" on current practices in media production and reception and also the technological apparatuses through which they are produced.

The visual array has always been impregnated with non-visual data (notated in various ways), but with the advent of technologies like electronic sensors/readers, GPS, RFID tags (etc.), we are now able to install — and have installed — information and infomatics into the spaces and objects in the cone of the visible; in a sense mediatising vision.

The news telescope draws on the fact that the visual is impregnated with non-visual data. Our "velo" of sight (veils of optical threads) is intersected by and may draw from matrices of information that lie "invisible" in the view (but are there nevertheless) into view. The "news telescope" is a located device which may be oriented and focused on different places and draw down different kinds of news from those places – setting them in contrast one to another. Thus, the demotic news of twitter feeds makes comment on traditional forms of news publication — organs of publication like newspapers. The "news telescope" places the news and asks the viewer to physically (and by extensión in other ways to) relate their place in the world to the places and different constructions of news.

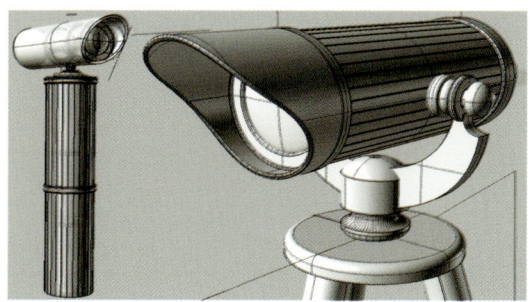

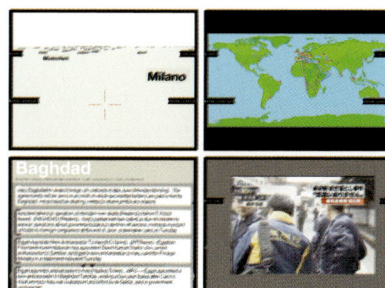

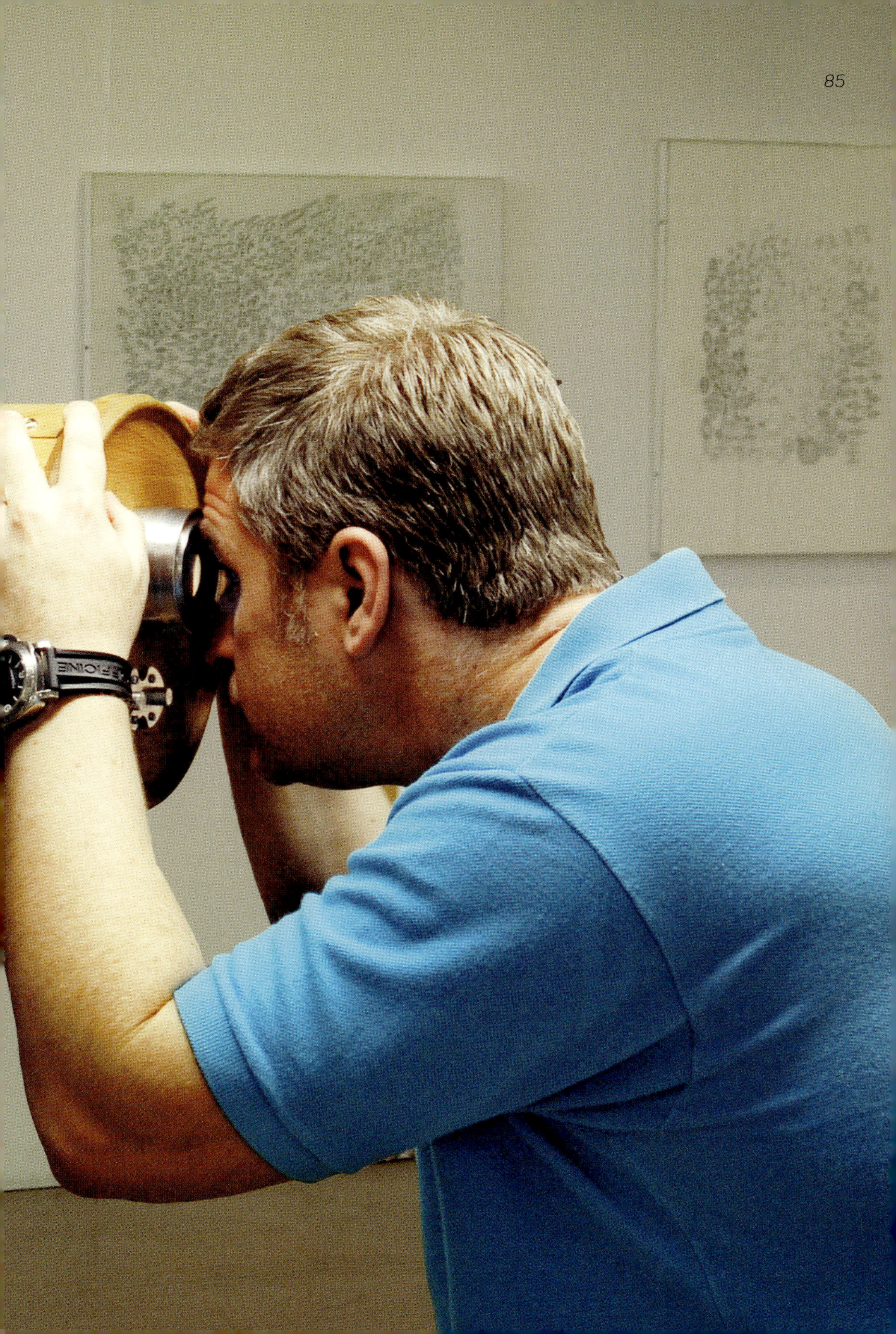

Human Activity
From the Renaissance to the 21st Century

In art history and archeology, as in any other branches of humanities, the increasing availability of massive amounts of quantitative data is fundamentally changing our perspective and research. Understanding impressive amounts of data — including bibliographies, inventory and research databases, Flickr images of historic sites, scanned books, click-streams of literature downloads, and other linked data is just as transformative for humanities, as the ideas of quantum mechanics were for physics in the beginning of the twentieth century.

In our hunt for general patterns and laws that characterize complex systems we find overarching themes, such as the one illustrated in figure 1, showing the reception of ancient Roman monuments in Western Renaissance documents (left), placed next to the the very same monuments as they appear in modern scholarly literature (right). The overall similarity between these two maps is obvious and rather amazing.

Both show that most documents (represented as brown nodes) depict or mention only a small number of monuments (given in blue), whereas a few documents point to a disproportionally large number of monuments, representing reviews or large catalogues. That is the reference patterns of art historians appear to follow the same hub dominated scale-free topology as the one characterizing the www, scientific citations, or the human cell. Another common feature is the fact that most nodes of the network are reachable from every other node with a very few hops. Obviously, these maps are driven by the interests, judgements and actions of each author who placed themselves on the map by referring to a shared core set of monuments, which allows for communication with peers, without a central control.

Albert László Barabási & Maximilian Schich

The equivalence of both maps is important, as it proves that old documents, which we consider subjects of our own study, behave just like the ones we produce today; in other words that the pattern of renaissance scholarship is very similar to our own present day effort in art history and archaeology. This has a number of consequences: First it allows us to simplify the way how we process and interpret data, as there is no need to view renaissance and modern scholarship as being fundamentally different. Second it fortifies the opinion that archaeology was not born thanks to the definitions of a single person in the 18th century, but emerged from the local and distributed activity of a large number of stakeholders. And finally it means that both our very own scholarly activity and the activity of our renaissance predecessors can be analyzed with the same tools.

Today we can produce maps such as those shown in the figure with incredible ease, offering a big picture that preserves the original source in its initial granularity, without being affected by filtering based on preconceived concepts or simplistic dissections of art history into stereotypic periods. Along these lines data driven research in the humanities, the social sciences and many other fields offers new insights every day, transforming our understanding of culture and society. As humanities, physics, biology and computer science join hands in subscribing to this new data driven approach, we are moving beyond the reductionist approaches of the past, providing a new understanding of the complexity of the world around us.

The data is taken from Census of Antique Works of Art and Architecture Known in the Renaissance. (ed. Arnold Nesselrath) Munich: Verlag Biering & Brinkmann 2005 URL: http://www.dyabola.de / now continued in http://www.census.de

FIG 1:

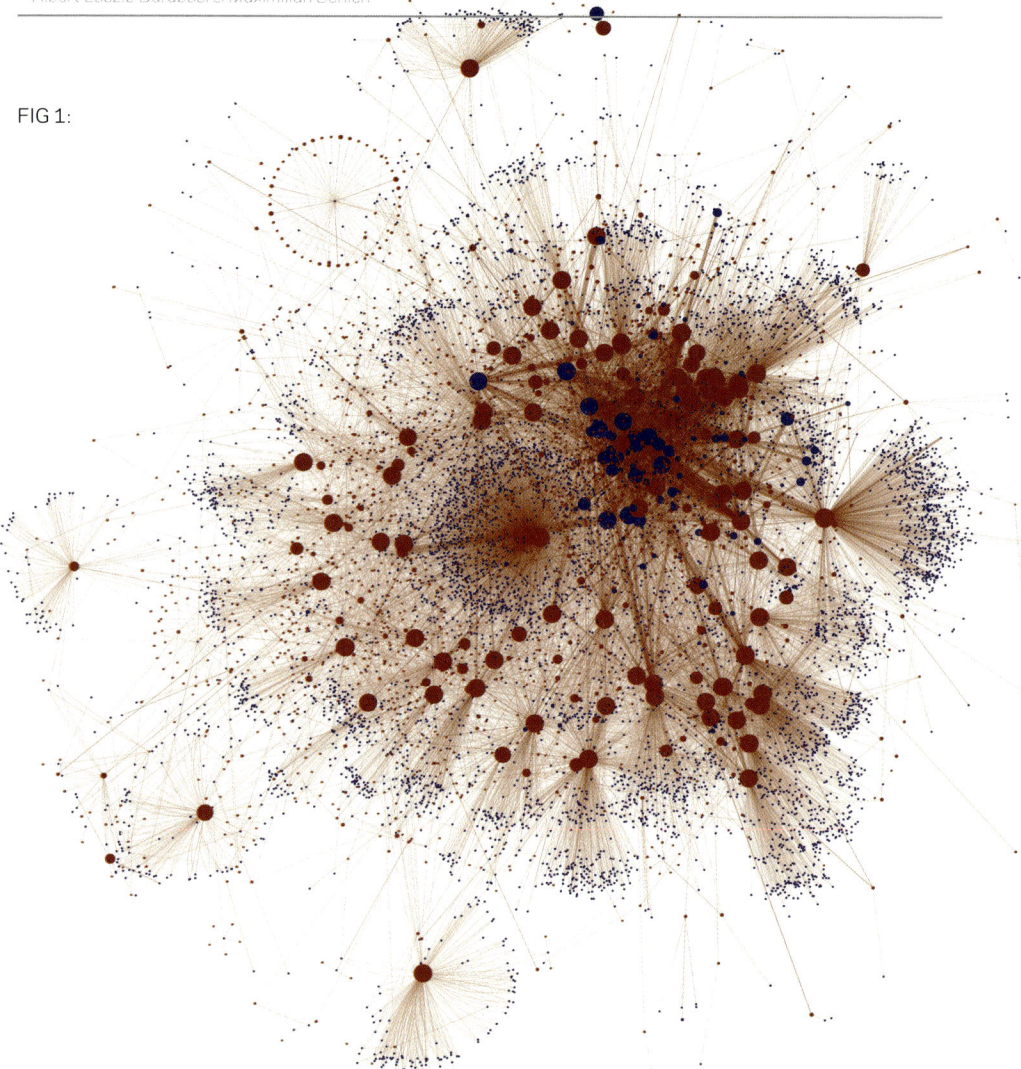

FIG 1: Reception of ancient monuments in western renaissance documents (left) and modern scholarly literature (right). Monuments are depicted as blue nodes; documents and literature are represented in brown. The node size indicates the number of subdivisions per nodes: documents range from single drawings to multivolume books; monuments include mostly sculptures and a few large buildings. The similarity of both maps shows that the perspectives of renaissance scholarship and modern art history and archaeology are equivalent.

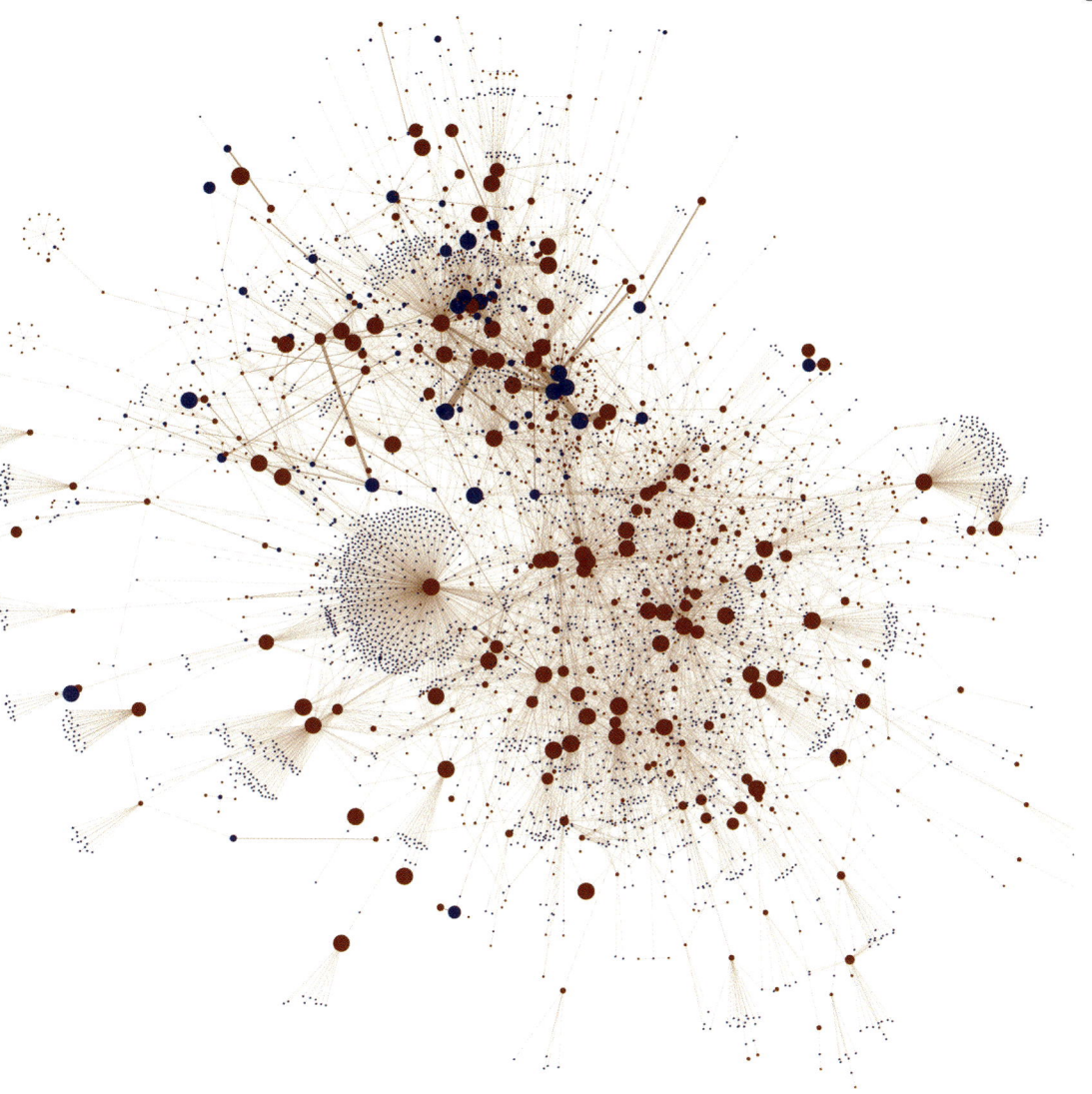

Curious Home
The Drift Table

**Interaction Research Studio,
Goldsmiths, University of London.**

The Drift Table allows people to float over the British landscape from the comfort of their own home. The weight of objects on the coffee table controls the slow scroll of high resolution photography displayed on a central view-port, giving detailed visual access to all of England and Wales. Adding weight causes the table both to accelerate and to descend towards the landscape below. But progress is always slow — travelling from London to Devon may take days. So what do you do with it? You do with it as you wish. The Drift Table is not designed to solve problems, but to provide a resource in the home. You might use it to take journeys, or to revisit favourite holiday destinations. You might explore particular questions about geography or town planning. You might even just lose yourself and watch the world go by.

Developed before the advent of systems like GoogleEarth™, the Drift Table can be seen as an investigation into new ways that information might enter the home. What are the implications of having access to terabytes of imagery as a mundane part of everyday life? Does it democratise information? Does it dissolve the boundaries of the home? The Drift Table also explores how we relate to digital technologies in everyday life. Should they always be task-oriented? What do we mean by usability? Perhaps most fundamentally, the Drift Table explores how designs can be left open for interpretation. The piece provides a rich resource for the home, but doesn't imply how it should be used — instead, it allows users to find their own meanings within it.

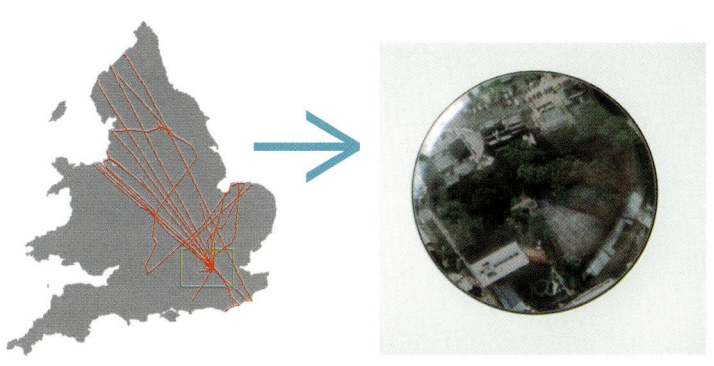

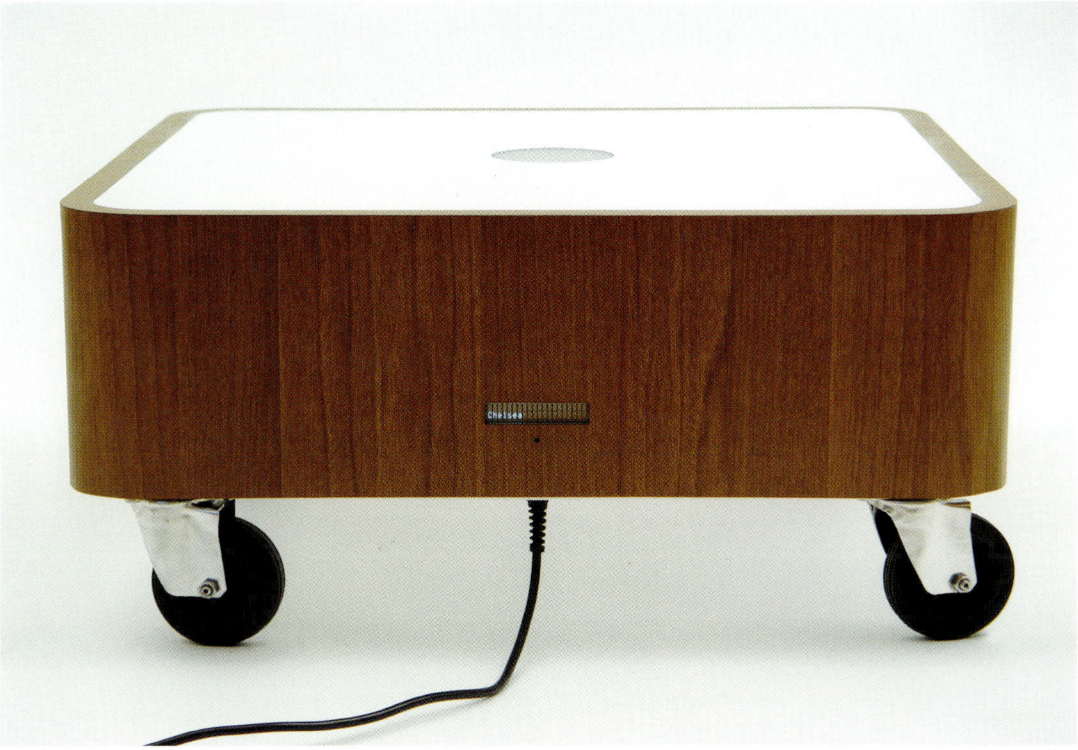

Open-ended designs like the Drift Table are completed by the ways people use them. We give our prototypes to people to live with for weeks and months. Ethnographic observation provides detailed information about how they accommodate the pieces, but we complement this with more experimental documentary videos produced by independent film-makers. These videos overlay meaning, showing users' own stories as fil-tered, edited and interpreted by the filmmakers. They serve as one facet in a multi-vocal account of our work.

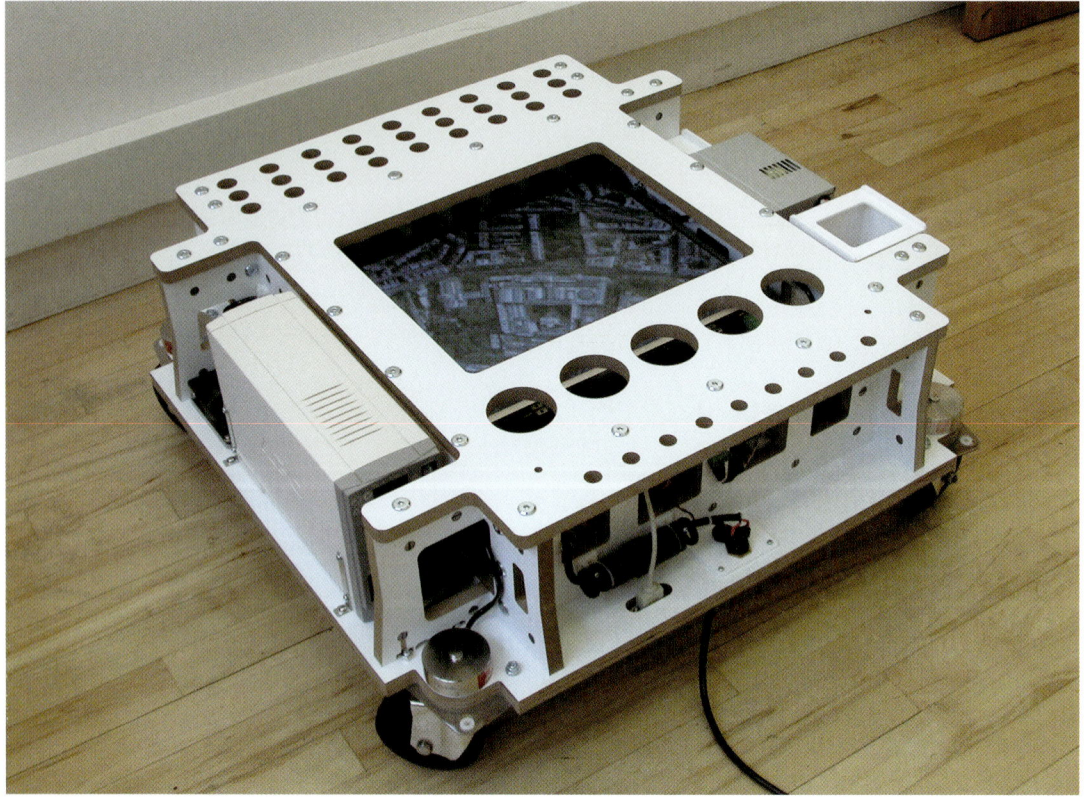

The Interaction Research Studio explores the design of computational systems for everyday life. Our practice-based research integrates design-led research methods with work on embedded and ubiquitous technologies to produce prototype products embodying new concepts for interaction. As an integral part of our process, we lend our prototypes to people to try in their everyday lives, with their stories becoming part of the designs.

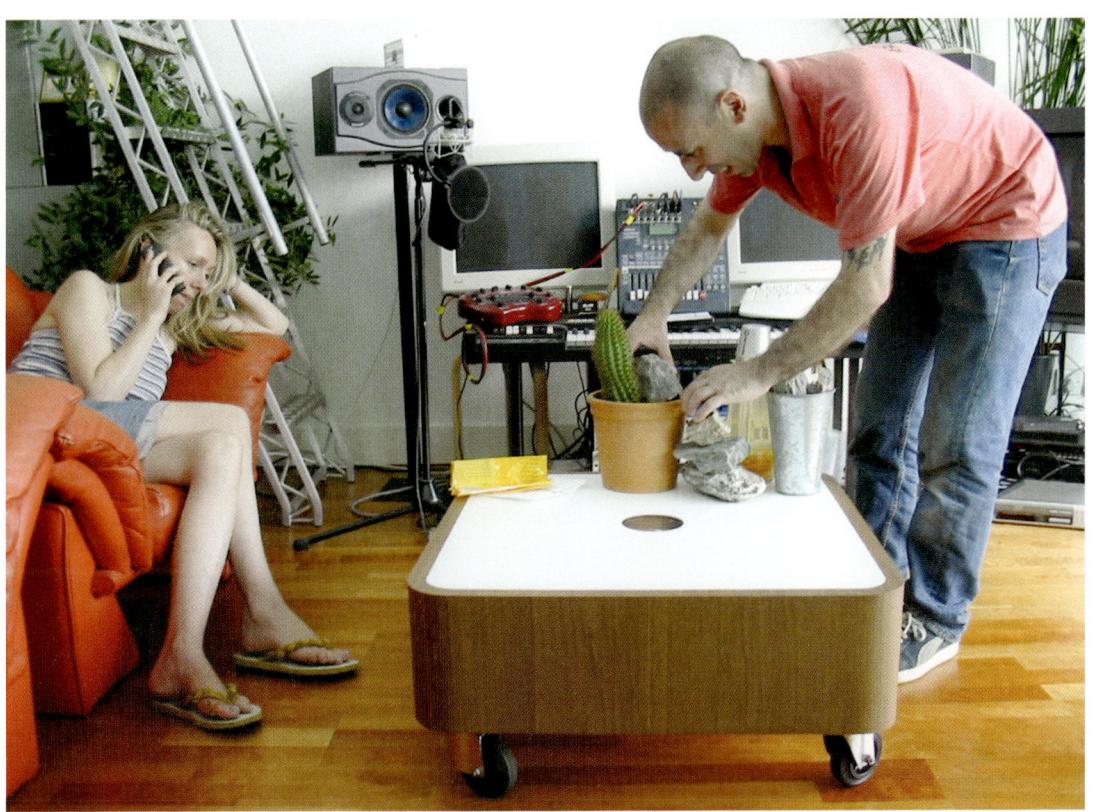

Temporality, Topology and Sociology

Sociology's time is both a resource and a topic. As a resource, sociologists perform time most obviously as a series of periods or epochs or eras. Accordingly, we emerged from the dark depths of the premodern into the (false) light of the modern, and now we meander in the murk of the late modern/high modern/postmodern. As a topic, time can, for instance, be studied in terms of different historical models of temporality: against the cyclical models of the premodern era (where the sense of time was grounded in diurnal and seasonal tempos) can be contrasted the linear models of modernity that are marked by progress, speed, acceleration. Alternatively, sociologists might study how the future is part of people's rhetorical arsenal: as we can only inhabit the present, the future is something we represent and circulate now in order to influence those whose actions will, hopefully, serve to realise the very future that we have painted. The practices of politicians, scientists, economists are characterised by contestations over the future: What is the future? How far away is it? What is the relevant unit of time (legislative session, financial year, interglacial period)? How fast are we moving towards it? Who or what is this 'we' (nation, region, globe)?

In all these sociological endeavours, the linear model of time predominates. Eras, and their respective models of time, are arrayed on a line extending from past to present to future; representations of the future (and the past) feed the rhetoric of the present as it rolls along.

The philosopher Michel Serres seems always to have worked topologically. He connects across disciplines and space and time (he detects chaos theory in Lucretius; in Zola, he finds intimations of thermodynamics). He eschews privileging one discipline or perspective over any another. Rather, he is interested in their inter-relations, how they connect, how they

Mike Michael

---

translate one another. His is a philosophy of prepositions and he has drawn on a range of concepts to capture these connections — Hermes, parasite, angels, quasi-object.

In light of this, how should we understand the recent interfacings of social science and topology? Certainly, we should not privilege one discipline's account. For instance, we should resist the temptation to view sociological recourse to topology through the sociological lens of professional differentiation and status hierarchies. Instead, this critical account can be folded into the exploration of those connections: where in the corpus of sociology do we find insinuations of the topological — perhaps in the figures of Simmel's stranger or Benjamin's angel of history? Of course, this point applies no less to topology. For instance, how do the concepts of the homeomorphic and homeotopic resonate with 'membership categorization devices' in conversation analysis?

With this move, we can also contribute to an alternative to the linear temporality assumed in a sociological account of the contemporary emergence of "topology in sociology." This "topology in sociology" is not simply about a new fashion, or a novel disciplinary tactic, or even intellectual progress. Each of these connotes some sort of advance on what went before: there is a not-so-tacit exercise of "critique" which is aligned with linear temporality. For Serres, "time flows in a turbulent and chaotic manner; it percolates....this time can be schematized by a kind of crumpling, a multiple, foldable diversity". In keeping with this topological model of time, the coming together of topology and sociology does not need to evoke advance or progress and the criticism of what went before, but a "multiple, foldable diversity", which might, ironically, indeed include critique.

The Web Starts Here
The IP Browser

Alex Galloway, Erik Borra, Michael Stevenson, Marieke van Dijk
& the Govcom.org Foundation, Amsterdam

Google has given us the ranked list of search engine returns. Librarians and editors provide directories, the Web categorized helpfully into topics. There is a third way of navigating the Web, still present in the "next blog" feature at blogspot.com, which also recalls early Web rings. This third way of browsing is also built into browsers, with their forward and back buttons. The IP Browser puts forward and back buttons onto the Web, more generally.

The IP Browser creates an alternative browsing experience that foregrounds the Web's machine habitat and returns the user back to the ba-

sics of orderly Web browsing. The IP Browser looks up your IP address, and allows you to browse the Websites in your IP neighborhood, one by one in the order in which they are given in the IP address space. The IP browser has a limited set of features: the user can either click to the next higher IP address or next lower one, using forward and backward buttons. Like a radio scanner, the browser skips over empty parts of the spectrum, incrementing the current IP address upward or downward until the next IP hosting a web service on port 80 is found. In this way, the user is able to browse specific IP address neighborhoods. The IP Browser re-contextualizes the Web as infrastructure within which websites are fit.

"The Web starts here — The IP Browser" is a Govcom.org Jubilee Production, 2008, session on alternative algorithms, led by Alexander Galloway. Programming by Erik Borra and design by Marieke van Dijk. Additional project participants include Rosa Menkman, Michael Stevenson and Laura van der Vlies.

The IP Browser is supported by Impakt Online, The Slow Web, Impakt Festival, Utrecht, 2009, www.impakt.nl/online. The IP Browser is online at ipbrowser.digitalmethods.net.

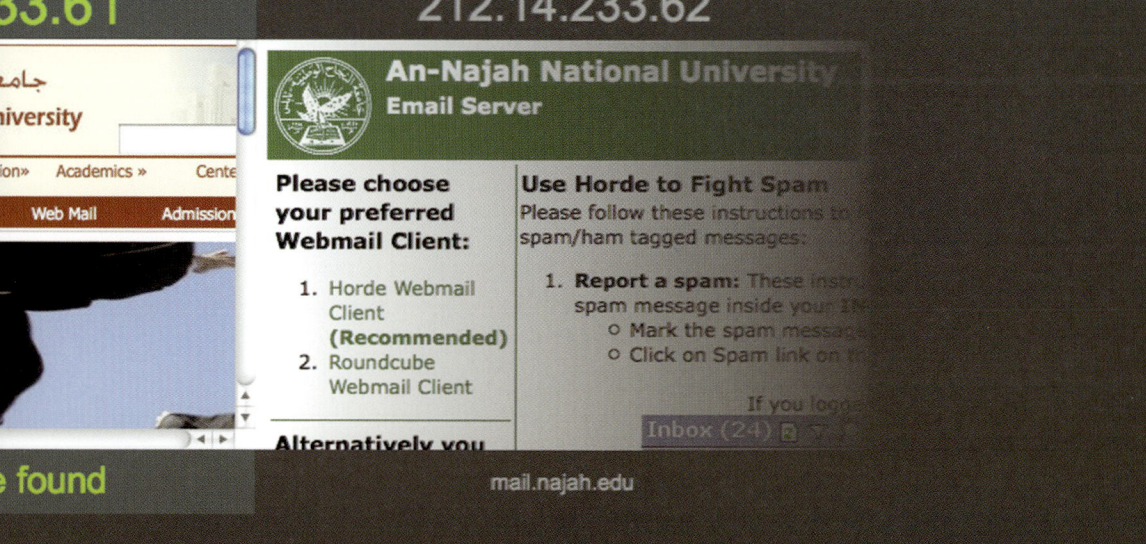

The Hidden Fragility of Complex Systems
Consequences of Change, Changing Consequences

Short-term survival and an exuberant plunge into building our future are generating a new kind of unintended consequence—hidden fragility. This is a direct effect of the sophistication and structural complexity of the socio-technical systems human's create.It is inevitable. And so the challenge is, How much can we understand and predict about these systems and about the social dynamics that lead to their construction?

Truly Complex Systems
Recent events cannot help but lead one to question the social environment and technological world we are constructing for ourselves.

After decades of building a new world economic order, the data is in: The Fall 2008 nearcollapse of the global financial system and its heart-wrenching impacts are empirical evidence that pure-market ideology does not work as a design principle for the world's economies. Historically, this design principle was justified in terms of the Efficient Market Hypothesis [Fama] — markets in their collective behavior will find the unique, optimal equilibrium condition that homogeneously maximizes human welfare. Sadly, this view is a theoretical artifact of experimentally ungrounded models. The mismatch between ideology and reality is desperately large.

The same design principles were championed in the corporate reorganization facilitated by the market deregulation movement over the same decades. Masquerading as concern for the shareholder, the lack of constraint resulted in new levels of mismanagement and a scale of market manipulation rare in history. The resulting instabilities led to the bankruptcies of Enron and World-Com; two examples of the "largest" (at the time) corporate collapses.

James P. Crutchfield

The lack of constraint did engender much creativity in financial instruments — a genuine efflorescence in the sophistication and level of abstraction operating in the world financial system. Aided and abetted by novel computing technologies, innovative strategies to reduce risk, to take one example, emboldened investment firms to over-reach using unusually large amounts of leverage. When the real markets did not meet the instruments' statistical-independence assumptions, the virtual wealth, on which the firms floated, simply evaporated.

For example, the innovation of portfolio insurance is implicated in "Black Monday" — the 19 October 1987 global stock market crash, which was the largest one-day percentage decline ever experienced, up to that time. A latent internal instability, automated in some markets with program trading, was amplified to global scale by the very mechanisms to "insure" investment portfolios. This hidden vulnerability was finally reified when a down-tick in the Hong Kong stock market grew through coupled international markets, spreading worldwide and causing an unprecedented and still somewhat mysterious crash.

Long Term Capital Management (LTCM), a hedge fund founded on just these kinds of financial innovations, provides yet another example. A very large (~100B) portfolio, heavily leveraged from 5B in assets, collapsed when relatively small variations in Russian markets revealed the lack of liquidity it required. Fearing the consequences of the firm's bankruptcy, LTCM was bailed out by its peers and the US Federal Reserve in 1998.

Now years later, these painful examples — Enron, WorldCom, LTCM, and the stock market on Black Monday — and others are almost entirely erased from our collective memory. Then again, perhaps they are particular cases, not worth remembering. Or do they have something to teach us about systems that we humans willfully construct to serve our needs? Their fragilities were unseen and unanticipated. Could they have been? Or is being blind-sided by our own creations inevitable? And, in any case, how are we to understand when our creations are so fragile?

Chagrined, it's nonetheless hard for us to miss the irony of good intentions. Financial instruments invented to reduce risk led to massive failures. To emphasize, innovations in managing risk produced risk on huge scales. And this observation leads us to our first puzzle. How is it that mechanisms on a small scale, with specific functioning and compelling benefits at that level, become exactly the drivers for catastrophic failure on the larger scale? Isn't this a contradiction? Doesn't a contradiction mean that such failures cannot happen? It may be a logical contradiction, but let's face the data from these seemingly accidental experiments. These constructed systems appear to have a dynamic that reshapes small-scale design into surprising, large-scale pattern. In any case, emergent contradiction appears to be fact. This is something to understand.

The basic architecture of fragility is not, as it happens, particular to financial systems. And this may be a good thing, in that a comparative view gives some hope of understanding what is going on. It turns out that many other large-scale engineered systems exhibit similar vulnerabilities.

The pre-9/11 air transportation system is a prime example. From volumes of regulatory, operating, and maintenance documents to the airplane themselves and the planet-spanning traffic routes, air transportation relies on many interlocking and coordinated subsystems. As a whole it is stunningly sophisticated, as are its components. That sophistication, though, means there are many levels of vulnerability. The sheer size of the network and passenger load preclude a centralized monitoring system. The planes themselves, highly evolved machines, are physically vulnerable to external attack and to the failure of only one of the many power and control systems required for them to operate. And, of course, both the transportation network and the planes are operated by humans who make mistakes. The net result is a system, on the one hand, on which economies have developed a dependence and, on the other, which is highly vulnerable to intentional disruption either by individuals (workers or terrorists). Air travel's very success translates into its being a target; its sophistication provides the leverage points for being co-opted. The events of 9/11 brought the air transportation system to its knees, inflicting heavy financial losses throughout the US economy.

The air transportation system in its success and planet-spanning organization has produced yet another kind of collateral fragility. The world health system is now more fragile than ever before and in unanticipated ways due to the rapid spread of epidemics through human-contact — contact that is accelerated by air transportation. The result is personal. Our health has become vulnerable to the arrival of once-distant, potentially virulent diseases; such as caused by the H1N1 virus that is now careering around the planet via international travel.

Despite collateral fragilities, we continue to craft much of modern life around such large-scale transport systems. Our homes and industries are powered via continent-scale electrical power distribution grids. From dozens of generation stations, spread over large geographic areas, each grid delivers its power synchronized to within tens of milliseconds. The very design requirements of long-range power-distribution and maintaining synchronization lead to a kind of coherence in behavior that leaves the grids vulnerable to large-scale failures. In such an architecture, the very strategies to mitigate localized failure, as we have repeatedly rediscovered, can lead through a cascade of cause-and-effect responses to major power outages. As it grows in size and sophistication, the power grid could become less, not more, stable.

So, are the goals and practice of engineering the source of vulnerabilities? No, hidden fragilities are not only the result of humans pursuing their needs. Nature herself is an analogous set of large-scale, interconnected systems. Natural systems are highly structured, being the long-lived products of competitive survival — the inheritance of evolution. And the interconnection between the system's are highly structured themselves, often for similar evolutionary reasons.

Climate change over the last several decades is an example of an interconnection between natural systems, particularly the atmosphere and oceans, and designed systems, such as transportation, power generation, agriculture, manufacturing, and extractive industries. The expected consequences of human-induced climate change are now a common-place: increasing mean global temperature, increasing local climatic variations, poleward movement of agriculture, drought, decreasing access to potable water, sea-level rise and coastal inundation, are some of the primary effects expected over the next century.

Humans are implicated in the systemic fragility that is climate change. This, however, need not be the case. For example, the recent wide-scale emergence of insect-driven deforestation suggests the appearance of a new stabilizing feedback loop that, independent of whether or not it originated through human activities, could very well become autonomous [ECC]. That is, such interconnected systems can innovate their own patterns which, in turn, lead to new fragilities. And, the patterns, having emerged and stabilized, can preclude mitigation.

At this point, we have a veritable zoo of systemic failures — failures in functioning, failures in design, and, certainly, failures in understanding. The list could be extended, too easily, to include the perceptual exaggerations induced by communications media, increasing economic dependence on the Internet, and the struggles for control mediated by policy-making institutions. Nonetheless, the examples given span a large enough range of system types that we can begin to see commonalities.

Understanding Truly Complex Systems

The world economy, financial markets, air transportation, pandemic disease spread, climate change, and insect-driven deforestation are examples of truly complex systems: They consist of multiple components, each component active in different domains and structured in its own right, interconnected in ways that lead to emergent collective behaviors and spontaneous architectural re-organization.

This is the world we built. Nation states maintain their survival and enhance their well being by participating in international trade. The degree of participation reflects the strength of coupling of their internal economies to the external world — the extent being a choice that balances internal needs and externally derived benefits. International trade is managed, in turn, at the largest scale via governmental negotiation, trade organizations, and global finance firms who rely on interconnected national financial markets. Internally, each state's financial system consists of a number of players, from national reserve and investment banks to insurance companies, institutiona investors, mortgage banks, and asset-based banks and workers. The real-economic component — materially productive industries and services — is supported by land, ocean, and air transportation systems. And this synopsis is only one slice. It says nothing of human culture and politics. The more one attempts to describe the social environment and technological systems we have constructed, the more complex they appear and the larger the mystery of their functioning becomes.

How are we to begin to understand truly complex systems and their hidden fragilities? Unfortunately, when it comes to considering how complex systems should be designed and should function, contemporary science and engineering, in their traditional positive and constructive role, largely miss the emergence of fragility. As one looks around in the (rather far-flung) literature, one finds models and results focused on rather the opposite — on the upsides of large-scale systems. There is a philosophy of boosterism for complicated systems: collaboration eclipses individual effort; the collective is more robust [Jen], smarter [Surowiecki], and tolerant [Carlson] than the local; economies are sustainable only if they grow; planet-scale geo-engineering will mitigate climate change. In short, after all these years and painful examples of failure, bigger is still better.

So what's going on? Why the mismatch between the reality of hidden fragility and the technooptimism that one sees driving science and engineering? We plunge head-long into our future, building socio-technical systems that are ever more complicated. Then, we are surprised when they fail so spectacularly.

Analyzing Fragility: Functional Pattern Formation

My premise is that truly complex systems, especially the socio-technical systems humans now construct, are inherently fragile. More to the point, they become so as a natural and inevitable product of how limited cognitive capacity, both at the individual and social levels, affects deploying technological solutions.

How does this happen? As they evolve, systems become more sophisticated — structurally more complex. That is, structural and behavioral correlation accumulates between components and across time. At face value, there is nothing problematic with this. It is a necessary part of building systems, as one commandeers new components and incorporates them, as they begin to work together. This is a simple, accretive view of the organization of complex systems in terms of a dynamic process through which they are created, either naturally, through human design, or both. The key and subtle step occurs, though, when the structural relationships between the components, specifically their dynamical interaction, leads to a spontaneous architectural reorganization as new levels of pattern emerge. That is, not only are individual components structurally complex and interconnected "horizontally" but, through evolution, they become nested [CalcEmerg,WEIR,EUC]. The new patterns represent an increased level of abstraction in the system and reflect increased correlation (more structure) at a new level of organization [Sem-Therm,OTMO]. This new level can take on its own functioning, stabilizing if reinforced by the system as a whole. I call this process functional pattern formation.

Functional pattern formation raises a difficulty, though. The naive assumption of the system being composed of "modules" — in particular, that the modules are structurally or dynamically independent — fails. When correlation spontaneously emerges, the original components no longer need be "modules." They interface in new ways within the system and can give rise to new, unanticipated behaviors and functions that cross the system. Moreover, these new functions can themselves become commandeered by other parts of the system. And, then, the entire process starting over again, with new levels of organization being constructed out of the existing ones. The lack of apparent modularity that results is the main challenge to understanding and analyzing truly complex systems.

In short, fragility emerges due to increasing structural correlation than spans system degrees of freedom and system degrees of abstraction. Fragility is hidden because it is emergent.

The argument here draws a connection between being "more structured" and being "more fragile." There is a list of technical conditions that must be met to rigorously translate from the former to the latter. Not all interventions or perturbations manifest fragility and lead to failure. Nonetheless, we intuitively appreciate the connection. We experience it all the time: Systems that are highly structured, complex in the sense I mean, are easy to destroy [Gould]. The long list of examples above reinforces the intuition, but at some point one must get down to brass tacks to test the hypothesis of fragility emerging through functional pattern formation. By what mechanisms does fragility emerge?

Lessons from Complex Systems

What can we learn from the contemporary study of complex systems and its tools, as found in nonlinear dynamics, patten formation theory, statistical mechanics, and the like?

The first general thing to note is that many of the observed behaviors of truly complex systems are perfectly consistent with the behaviors and organizations that general systems can produce.

This could not be said three centuries ago. Prior to the modern era of complex systems, the behavior of the example systems above could only be interpreted as due to pure chance or, in effect, as not having a mechanistic explanation. We now know better. Complex systems have particular internal mechanisms that can be modeled and whose workings are understood. An important side result is that we also now know that there are strict limits to what can be predicted.

For example, one of the earliest lessons from complex systems is the existence of deterministic chaos — perfectly deterministic systems that over the long-term generate complicated and random seeming behavior. It turns out that there are a number of important properties of chaotic systems which underlie hidden fragility.

One is the exponential amplification of small effects. In the present case — networked systems with many degrees of freedom and many layers of organization — this sensitivity manifests itself as the rapid propagation of information across the system. Above, this was referred to as failures that cascade across system components.

Yet another consequence is that impending failure has a signature. In particular, as a system reorganizes itself from one stable behavioral regime to another, following the process of functiona pattern formation, fluctuations and noise will be amplified. That is, to exchange the stability of one kind of behavior for another, the system must pass through a condition of neutral stability.

There, external perturbations filter more easily through the system, whose behaviors will fluctuate more wildly than before or after the transition.

One general consequence of deterministic chaos — unlike the above, a limitation — is that component interconnections and internal nonlinearities typically mean that most emergent properties, including fragility, cannot be predicted in advance [CalcEmerg,NeverDie]. In this case, one appeals to model building and simulation to ferret out the emergent properties. Or, one even appeals to new methods to automate this process [EoMfaDS]. To the extant one can recast the overt complexity in a model, the better the position from which to understand, forecast, and intervene.

Another, somewhat different insight from complex systems is more recent and addresses the collective behavior of groups of intelligent agents. Curiously, when intelligence is added to agents the group behavior tends to become more complicated and, in some cases, chaotic. Why? At first blush, agent intelligence is good. It allows for increased memory and sophisticated strategies. The result. though, is that, by anticipating each others' moves, agents start to "chase" each other's changing strategies. The group behavior starts to oscillate; when, in contrast, simpleminded agents would or could not adapt dynamically. Technically stated, dynamical systems consisting of adaptive agents typically do not tend to a mutually beneficial global condition — they cannot find the Nash Equilibrium [Sato/JPC]. The lesson is that dynamical instability is inherent to collectives of adaptive agents.

A key step in understanding complex systems in monitoring how structured they are. In the case of functional pattern formation, the amount of structure increases and one needs to be able to measure this. Computational mechanics [ISC,CalcEmerg,CMPPSS] gives a way to define and measure the degree of organization of a complex system by answering three questions: (i) How much historical information does a system store, (ii) In what architecture is that information stored, and (iii) How is the stored information used to produce future behavior? The temporal evolution of these measures is itself a useful diagnostic for truly complex systems, especially those that through evolution and adaptation build up internal structures and increase in fragility.

The truly complex systems described above can be analyzed along these lines. Better than giving a detailed explication here, though, is to listen to an earlier voice. The philosopher Alfred North Whitehead captured the essential character of evolving, adapting systems most elegantly, when in the 1920s he considered the domain of human social organization [Whitehead]:

"The social history of mankind exhibits great organizations in their alternating functions of conditions for progress, and of contrivances for stunting humanity. The history of the Mediterranean lands, and of western Europe, is the history of the blessing and the curse of political organizations, of religious organizations, of schemes of thought, of social agencies for large purposes. The moment of dominance, prayed for, worked for, sacrificed for, by generations of the noblest spirits, marks the turning point where the blessing passes into the curse. Some new principle of refreshment is required. The art of progress is to preserve order amid change, and to preserve change amid order. Life refuses to be embalmed alive. The more prolonged the halt in some unrelieved system of order, the greater the crash of the dead society."

Whitehead also saw parallels in the temporal evolution of structural complexity (and its aesthetic appreciation) in the cognitive-social dynamics of fashion [Whitehead]:

"The same principle is exhibited by the tedium arising from the unrelieved dominance of fashion in art. Europe, having covered itself with treasures of Gothic architecture, entered upon generations of satiation. These jaded epochs seem to have lost all sense of that particular form of loveliness. It seems as though the last delicacies of feeling require some element of novelty to relieve their massive inheritance from bygone system. Order is not sufficient. What is required, is something much more complex. It is order entering upon novelty; so that the massiveness of order does not degenerate into mere repetition; and so that the novelty is always reflected upon a background of system."

There is a cyclic signature: building up organization that, stabilized, becomes substrate for further innovation, but that, aging, converts to constraint against adaptation, eventually leading to collapse from its very own benefits. It parallels the failure dynamic exhibited by our truly complex systems. One cannot also help but draw parallels with the structural adaption of renewal seen in ecological succession [Holling] and hoped for in the "business cycle."

Looking Forward

Faced with the increasingly complex socio-technical systems that we collectively build, it is perhaps not hopeful to conclude that fragility is endemic and, worse, that the process which creates it, hides it. Nonetheless, I am hopeful, since the concepts and techniques of complex systems are up to the task of understanding and analyzing hidden fragility.

Hopeful, that is, but for one thing. There is a nagging concern that the public sphere is unable to support the sophisticated discourse required to democratically stop creating the conditions for fragility. In other words, the public sphere, itself a truly complex system, does not have sufficient structural complexity. Specifically, I am optimistic due the available mathematical tools and future likely technical advances. I am less sanguine about how that understanding will be translated into action through political and public processes.

Fortunately, there are hints of increasing self-awareness on the part of the players in some of the domains discussed here. For example, Nobel Laureate Paul Krugman's re-evaluation of the goals and foundations of economics are heartening [Krugman]. Also in the financial sphere, fragility is eginning to receive attention [Bookstaber]. In the climate domain, there is increasing appreciation of complex-systems subtleties in the recent attention paid to sudden climate shifts [Schwartz]: Not all change is gradual and proportionate.

These glimmers are just the beginning. Especially so, if we are to understand the apparent commonality across the truly complex systems discussed here. A more substantial push is needed for a general theory of complex systems. Of late, in response to criticisms of too much abstraction, the field has taken a respite from this difficult task to focus on disseminating its tools through applications. Now it is time to turn back to the search for general principles. The challenges will not be met by only studying particular cases; conceptual innovation is required. This is particularly necessary, since many of the problems confronting us require action — we will have to intervene. And this brings in a whole new level of understanding how to control complex systems. Of similar importance is understanding time-dependent control or, what above was called, "adaptation." This topic sorely needs attention. We will also require new tools to manage the vast amounts of data that we can (and should) be collecting from truly complex systems. For example, we need new tools that automate building models, analyzing hierarchical organization, and monitoring fragility [EoMfaDS]. Finally, What is the role of experiment in building our complex socio-technical systems? To date, little or none. But we are clearly engaged, if accidentally, in experimentation. So, at least, we could take better data. This would provide some solace, perhaps only to a vanishingly small degree, for the suffering that follows when our systems fail.

This essay is based on a talk "Terrorizing Complex Systems" presented at the Santa Fe Institute to the Business Network Topical Meeting on "Modeling Terrorism as a Complex n Santa Fe, New Mexico, 10 April 2003. It has been updated to include illustrative events since that time. (The talk PDF is available at http://cse.ucdavis.edu/~chaos/chaos/talks.htm.)

References

— [ISC] J. P. Crutchfield and Karl Young, "Inferring Statistical Complexity", *Physical Review Letters* 63 (1989) 105-108.

— [NeverDie] J. P. Crutchfield, "Is Anything Ever New? Considering Emergence", in Complexity: *Metaphors, Models, and Reality*, G. Cowan, D. Pines, and D. Melzner, editors, Santa Fe Institute Studies in the Sciences of Complexity XIX (1994) 479-497.

— [EoMfaDS] J. P. Crutchfield and B. S. McNamara, "Equations of Motion from a Data Series", *Complex Systems*, 1 (1987) 417-452.

— [Fama] E. F. Fama, "Efficient Capital Markets—A Review of Theory and Empirical Work", *Journal of Finance* 25:2 (1970) 383-417.

— [CalcEmerg] J. P. Crutchfield, "The Calculi of Emergence: Computation, Dynamics, and Induction", *Physica* D 75 (1994) 11-54.

— [ECC] D. Dunn and J. P. Crutchfield, "Entomogenic Climate Change: Insect Bioacoustics and Future Forest Ecology", *Leonardo* 42:3 (June 2009) 239-244.

— [EUC] J. P. Crutchfield and E. van Nimwegen, "The Evolutionary Unfolding of Complexity", in *Evolution as Computation: DIMACS Workshop, Princeton, 1999*, L. F. Landweber and E. Winfree, editors, Natural Computing Series, Springer-Verlag, New York (2002) 67-94.

— [WEIR] James P. Crutchfield, *"When Evolution is Revolution. Origins of Innovation"*, in *Evolutionary*

Dynamics. Exploring the Interplay of Selection, Neutrality, Accident, and Function, J. P. Crutchfield and P. K. Schuster, editors, Santa Fe Institute Series in the Sciences of Complexity, Oxford University Press, Oxford, United Kingdom (2001) 101-133.

— [Whitehead] A. N. Whitehead, *Process and Reality (Gifford Lectures Delivered in the University of Edinburgh During the Session 1927-28)*, Free Press, second edition (1979).

— [OTMO] J. P. Crutchfield and O. Gornerup, "Objects That Make Objects: The Population Dynamics of Structural Complexity", *J. Roy. Soc. Interface* 3 (2006) 345-349.

— [Holling] L. H. Gunderson, C. S. Holling, and S. S. Light, *Barriers and Bridges to Renewal of Regional Ecosystems and Institutions*. Columbia University Press, New York (1995).

Holling, C.S., "Simplifying the complex: The paradigms of ecological function and structure", *European Journal of Operational Research 30* (1987) 139-146.

— [Krugman] P. Krugman, "How did Economists Get It So Wrong?", *New York Times Magazine*, (6 September 2009) MM36.

— [Schwartz] P. Schwartz and D. Randall, "An Abrupt Climate Change Scenario and Its Implications for United States National Security", (October 2003).

— [Bookstaber] R. Bookstaber, "A Demon of Our Own Design: Markets, Hedge Funds, and the Perils of Financial Innovation", Wiley, New York (2007).

— [Jen] E. Jen, Robust Design: *A Repertoire of Biological, Ecological, and Engineering Case Studies*, Oxford University Press (2004).

— [Surowiecki] J. Surowiecki, "The Wisdom of Crowds", Random House, New York (2004).

— [Carlson] J. Carlson and J. Doyle, "Complexity and Robustness", *Proceedings of the National Academy of Sciences* USA 99:1 (2002) 2538-2545.

— [Gould] S. J. Gould, "The Great Asymmetry", Science 279:5352 (1998) 812-813.

For the ppl of Iran: #iranelection RT

Richard Rogers, Esther Weltevrede, Erik Borra, Marieke van Dijk & the Digital Methods initiative, Amsterdam

Twitter, generally, and also during the Iran election crisis (June 2009 and beyond), has been described as banal. The question is, could the hundreds of thousands of tweets about the Iran election crisis be made into a comprehensible account of what has been happening on the ground as well as online? "For the ppl of Iran – #iranelection RT," is such an attempt. The project, first, is a stored collection of all the tweets that have been tagged #iranelection from the first one on 10 June up to 30 June 2009, some 650,000 in all. The top three "retweeted" tweets (RTs) per day have been filtered and organized chronologically, as opposed to the reverse chronology that Twitter uses. The resulting output is a capsule account of the crisis, which also was subsequently edited, and made into sub-storylines, on arrests, violence, Neda, censorship as well as the Internet.

"For the ppl of Iran – #iranelection RT" tells the story of the day-to-day unfolding of the Iran election crisis as seen through Twitter. The top retweets show the urgency and emotion of those twenty days in June, when the tensions on the streets and the coverage in the media were at their height. The crisis unfolds on Twitter with the discovery of the value of the #iranelection hash tag, and tweeters both in and outside Iran begin using the tag to mark all tweets about the events there. Mousavi holds an emergency press conference. The voter turn-out is 80%. SMS is down; Mousavi's website and Facebook are blocked. Police are using pepper spray. Mousavi is under house arrest, and declares he is prepared for martyrdom. Neda is dead. There is a riot in Baharestan Square. First aid info is here. Bon Jovi sings "Stand by Me" in support. Ahmadinejad is confirmed the winner. Light a candle for the ppl of Iran.

The collection of tweets also shows how tweeters respond to what is happening online and on the ground. Tweets reporting blocked websites are followed up by proxy offers. Accounts of police using pepper spray are followed up by links to websites with first aid information.

"For the ppl of Iran — #iranelection RT" is an exercise in transforming the supposed banality of Twitter into a machine that recounts events on the ground and in social media.

About the #iranelection collection of tweets (10-30 June 2009)

— Tweets tagged with #iranelection: **653,883**
— Unique number of Twitter users using #iranelection tag: **99,811**
— Number of Twitter users using #iranelection with multiple tweets: **46,702**
— Number of Twitter users using #iranelection with greater than 20 tweets: **6,000**
— Number of Twitter users using #iranelection with 1 tweet: **53,109**
— Number of Twitter users using #iranelection who were retweeted: **36,913**
— Number of Twitter users using #iranelection who were retweeted multiple times: **16,336**
— Number of Twitter users using #iranelection who were retweeted 10 times or more: **2,829**
— Number of Twitter users using #iranelection who were retweeted 1 time: **20,577**
— Number of languages in #iranelection: **26**
— Number of tweets in #iranelection in English: **612,373**
— Number of tweets in #iranelection in Farsi: **6,248**

"For the ppl of Iran — #iranelection RT" is a production of the Digital Methods Initiative, Summer School, 2009, session on media attention formats, led by Richard Rogers. Programming by Erik Borra, design by Marieke van Dijk and editorial by Kimberley Spreeuwenberg and Esther Weltevrede. #iranelection RT is online at http:// www.rettiwt.net/ (request login at issuecrawler.net).

#iranelection RT Top 3 retweets per day

Jun 10   Wow - Twitter search can let you see all the Iran election tweets coming out of Tehran http://bit.ly/x5C8P #IranElection 3 retweets   Prosecutor General declares unequal airtime given to candidates is against the law http://bit.ly/1bhCHk #IranElection 2 retweets   Mousavi boycotts TV debate due to unfair time allocation: 20 min to Ahmadinejad, 1:41 to Mosuavi #IranElection

 2 retweets   Jun 11   RT@LaraABCNewsAhmedinejad = Bush, Mousavi = #Obama? Sadjadpour's neat analysis of #iranelection http://bit.ly/14jy0Y 4 retweets   Marc Lynch asks "Could there be a Mousavi Effect?" http://bit.ly/12hkAW #IranElection #retweet_thursday 4 retweets   RT: @alexlobov: RT @keyvan Expect internet connection problems and new wave of filtering in Iran within next 72 hours. #IranElection 3 retweets   Jun 12   Mousavi will hold emergency press conference in 15 mins in Tehran http://havadaran.net/archive/00309.php #IranElection 6 retweets   My conclusions after seeing 100s of #IranElection photos: Tehran looks a lot like Tel-Aviv and ALL Iranian girls are beautiful 5 retweets   Reports says more that 80% are electing. This is very high, first time in the history of islamic republic #iranelection 5 retweets   Jun 13   Latest photos from Tehran: www.flickr.com/mousavi1388/ (updated every minute) #IranElection 11 retweets   Mousavi has been arrested!!!!!! http://tr.im/oopK #iranelection 11 retweets   SMS is down, Moussavi's websites and Facebook are filtered, state TV is celebrating and people are in the streets. #IranElection

 10 retweets   Jun 14   PLEASE RT (ReTweet) these pictures http://twitpic.com/7c85l AND http://ow.ly/e11H and this hashtag 348 retweets   Dear Iranian People, Mousavi has not left you, he has been put under house arrest by Ministry of Intelligence #IranElection 80 retweets   #iranelection We witnessed police spraying pepper gas into the eyes of peaceful female protesters 36 retweets

Jun 15   Functioning Iran proxies 218.128.112.18:8080 218.206.94.132:808 218.253.65.99:808 219.50.16.70:8080 #iranelection 410 retweets   Our Iranian friends can access Twitter from 148.233.239.24 Port:80 in Tehran. Can avoid govt filters from here. #iranelection 131 retweets   to other sources: this isn't the police! police is still outside! we're under attack by Ansar-Hezbolah. #iranelection 67 retweets   Jun 16   Twitter Reschedules Maintenance Around #IranElection Controversy http://bit.ly/2xWNy (via 223 retweets   RT From Iran: CONFIRMED!! Army moving into Tehran against protesters! PLEASE RT! URGENT! #IranElection 222 retweets   RT Open Letter to the World from the People of Iran: http://tinyurl.com/nw95ev Please RT. 129 retweets   Jun 17   Simple ways to help Iranian free speech: http://is.gd/13U0V #IranElection #gr88 Pls RT

 536 retweets   RT from Iran: #IranElection Regime still pretending there's no protest outside Tehran RT this HUGE demo pic NOW- http://twitpic.com/7ki6e 250 retweets   U.S. Government Asks Twitter to Stay Up for #IranElection Crisis . http://bit.ly/5Cade 116 retweets   Jun 18   RT Add your username to the Green Wall to show support for #iranelection http://iran.greenthumbnails.com 272 retweets   Mindblowing #IranElection Stats: 221,744 Tweets Per Hour at Peak http://bit.ly/3xmvpE 209 retweets   to protect us all followers pls change your twt location to IRAN GMT+3.30 - #Iranelection RT RT RT 69 retweets   Jun 19   MOUSAVI APPEALS TO THE WORLD TO PARTICIPATE IN SEA OF GREEN IN IN ALL CAPITAL CITIES THIS SUNDAY #Iranelection RT RT RT - confirmed 108 retweets   RT From Iran: "I have one vote. I gave it to Moussavi. I have one life. I will give it for Freedom." #IranElection 59 retweets   RT from Iran: The

situation in Iran is now CRITICAL - the nation is heartbroken - suppression is iminent - #Iranelection

52 retweets `Jun 20` I am prepared For martyrdom, go on strike if I am arrested #IranElection

174 retweets Courage! Please, please, read this short piece & RT: http://bit.ly/IQUI5 #IranElection

70 retweets STOP supporting US backed coup in Iran. #IranElection #IranElection 64 retweets

`Jun 21` RT If an innocent girl gets shot halfway across the world, does she make a sound? Yes, and the whole world hears her. #IranElection 117 retweets RT "On 9/11, the world said we were all Americans. Tonight, we're all Iranian" #IranElection #Neda 79 retweets RT RT WIDELY FIRST AID INFO IN FARSI: مکشلزبشیک http://gr88.tumblr.com/ #IranElection 68 retweets `Jun 22` PLEASE RT: THIS IS WHY WE PROTEST. @ http://digg.com/d1uPU9 #iran #iranelection 462 retweets Anonymous secure blog RT bypass govt. blocks Free Select Canada to auto-download http://tinyurl.com/nzxco5 #iranelection 188 retweets Help Iran free speech. RT. Anonymous web tool. Free. Select country Canada http://tinyurl.com/nzxco5 #iranelection 119 retweets `Jun 23` RT MOUSAVI Declares ALL IRAN STRIKE TUESDAY & Rest of Week! Do NOT WORK! STAY HOME OR PROTEST! Close ALL Bazaars! #IranElection #N 64 retweets #iranelection RT http://iran.greenthumbnails.com/ learn, understand, support 57 retweets FREE SPEECH! DO NOT SUPPORT BLOODY COUP IN IRAN! #IranElection Tehran http://tinyurl.com/m7w4pg 56 retweets

`Jun 24` New pictures of Neda along with a profile of her life http://bit.ly/14ebTK #neda 64 retweets in Baharestan we saw militia with axe choping ppl like meat - blood everywhere - like butcher - Allah Akbar - #Iranelection 62 retweets they pull away the dead into trucks - like factory no human can do this - we beg Allah for save us - #Iranelection 61 retweets `Jun 25` RT URGENT FOR WOUNDED!! English & FARSI FIRST AID INFO: (http://gr88.tumblr.com/) #Iranelection 102 retweets RT Please RT Video June 24th Riot in Baherstan Sq. posted today http://bit.ly/Hrh71 #iranelection 87 retweets Plz send your videos to for media, esp CNN. When filming show newspaper to prove date. Very Imp RT RT RT #iranelection 36 retweets `Jun 26` RT - natarsim natarsim ma hame ba ham hastim - Don't be afraid, don't be afraid. We are all in this together #IranElection #iran 40 retweets Doctor who was with Neda in her last moments took a risk to speak to BBC: http://tinyurl.com/nrrg63 30 retweets Statistical analysis suggests fraud in #iranelection http://bit.ly/63MKI 22 retweets `Jun 27` God is Great #Iranelection #revolution #neda RT RT RT everybody 70 retweets RT Please RT Video June 24th Riot in Baherstan Sq. http://bit.ly/Hrh71 #iranelection #gr88 32 retweets Check out the new tribute video for #iranelection. Dedicated to those protesting in Iran. Amazing video.RT RT RT http://tinyurl.com/lqpxvv 28 retweets

`Jun 28` British embassy staff arrested in Iran, Foreign Office confirms http://bit.ly/6jjnP #iranelection 66 retweets Iran government TV: Eight local British embassy staffers arrested http://bit.ly/13hAZ8 #iranelection 28 retweets has been arrested. Some solidarity might not go amiss. RT! #iranele 20 retweets `Jun 29` Bon Jovi, Andy Madadian & Richie S. sing "Stand By Me" 2 support #iranelection http://tr.im/q3hj 88 retweets #Neda (You Will Not Defeat The People) #music video 4 neda and the ppl of Iran 50 retweets Bon Jovi & Iranian Superstar Andy M. sing "Stand By Me" 2 support #iranelection http://tr.im/q3hj RT 47 retweets `Jun 30` RT Support your local Iranians! Only shop at 7-11. FREE IRAN!! ... with purchase of any medium size slurpee... #iranelection 75 retweets RT Ahmadinejad WINS!!! Everyone else can SUCK IT!!!! #iranelection 25 retweets RT Please LIGHT a CANDLE for those who have DIED! PLZ RT! #iranelection Iran #Neda 6 retweets

Network Topology: a Tendency to Differ

"…all innovative, creative systems are divergent, conversely, sequences of events that are predictable are, ipso facto, convergent"[1]

The communication topology of Empire is complex as it is woven together by airplanes, freight ships, television, cinema, computers, and telephony, but what all these different systems seem to have in common is their convergence on the figure not simply of the network, but a kind of *hypernetwork*, a meshwork of networks potentially connecting every point to every other point. As such, the network is becoming less and less a description of a specific system as a catchword to describe the formation of a single and yet multi-dimensional information milieu — linked by the dynamics of information propagation and segmented by diverse modes and channels of circulation…. (U)nlike the other global communication technologies mentioned above, it has been conceived and evolved as a *network of networks*, or an inter-network, a topological formation that presents some challenging insights into the dynamics underlying the formation of a global network culture. As a technical system, the Internet consists of a set of interrelated protocols, little abstract technical diagrams that give the network consistency beyond the rapidly changing hardware environment of computers, servers, cable and wires. Even as basic Internet protocols have been changed over time, the philosophy that has informed their design and hence the architecture of the Internet has been consistent overall and informed by a few key principles which have, up until this moment, survived scalability (such as a universal address space, a layered and modular structure, the distributed movements of data packets and the interoperability of heterogeneous systems). Such principles imply a strong conception of an informational milieu as a dynamic topological formation,

Tiziana Terranova

---

characterized by a tendency to divergence and differentiation, posing the problem of *compatibility* and the production of a *common space* as an active effort involving an unstable or metastable milieu. In other words, beyond being a concrete assemblage of hardware and software, the inter-network is also an abstract technical diagram implying a very specific pro-duction of space. ...what characterizes the technical diagram and design principles that have driven the development of the Internet is a tendency to understand space in terms of the bio-physical properties of *open sys-tems*. By modeling such open network spatiality the Internet becomes for us more than simply one medium among many, but a kind of general figure for the processes driving the globalization of culture and communication at large.

[...]

What makes the Internet a challenging medium is not only the nature of its technological components but more generally the design principles that have informed its ongoing evolution. The Internet, in fact, is not just a global computer network, but a network of networks, the actualization of a set of design principles entailing the inter-operability of heterogeneous information systems. Not only, that is, there is no central control of the Internet (although there are many control centers), but the whole space of communication has been designed and conceived in terms of dynamic and variable relations between different communication networks[2]. The Internet was conceived from its inception as a heterogeneous network, able to ac-commodate in principle if not in actuality, not only diverse communication systems, but also drifting and differentiating communication modes.

[...] The development of internetworking technologies is crucially concerned with modulating the relationship between differentiation and universality[...]Command functions need to be distributed, thus allowing a communication network to survive the destruction of a high percentage of its nodes. At the same time, such distribution of command functions once applied to a system that is conceived as always potentially open to new additions carries within itself a tendency to divergence and differentiation that in the absence of a coherent design strategy can easily lead to catastrophic transformations (such as the breakdown of the network in secluded territories). Subtracted from the central controlling gaze of a single centre, space tends not so much to fragment into individual cells, but to diverge, hybridizing itself around the peculiar features of different milieus and cultures. Decentralized and distributed networks, although intrinsically more robust and resilient than centralized ones, present the intrinsic problem of a tendency to differentiation and drift that threatens to turn the open network into an archipelago of disconnected and isolated islands.

This tendency of decentralized networks to diverge to the point of disconnection is named by open architecture as a tendency towards the production of *incompatibilities*. Divergence brings with it the tendency to disconnection and disconnection produces incompatibilities. The adaptability and flexibility inherent in the shift away from expensive mainframes towards micro-computers and eventually personal computers makes computer networks particularly liable to modifications and mutations, to specialized uses inherent to the multiplicity of contexts to which computing spreads.

[...]

To say that sociologists and cultural theorists have tended to overlook the duration of electronic space does not mean that the study of network dynamics is a neglected field. While sociologists and philosophers have thoroughly debated the relation between space and time in network societies, mathematicians and physicists have been busy modeling the dynamic of Internet traffic and its relation to the topology of cyberspace. What the former mostly see as a single electronic space causing a time-space implosion, the latter see as the epiphenomenal manifestation of hidden physical laws that make the Internet part of a more general class of bio-physical systems. On the one hand, a technology implicated in the social collapse of distances, the imperialist homogenization of times, and the reduction of the heterogeneity of the world to the one dimension of communication. On the other hand, a type of dynamical physical system characterized by a specific topological distribution, whose laws must be discovered and formalized. In between these different visions of the network, lies the sprawl of Internet culture….

Internet culture has thus given us some important topoi of network space, able to capture and impart a specific speed and consistency to the potential indeterminacy of information flows. We have had boards and domains, lists and webs, but also spheres and rings binding local areas of connectivity within an open information space. These figures express the power of a local movement able to bind the turbulence of the flows within a new type of informational structure. If Bulletin Board System offered a steady platform from where to launch oneself onto an open info-space, the fragmentation of web space that favors the power of attraction of the portals is counteracted by web-rings, where small sites with similar content form a circular vortex able to capture and channel the attention of the web surfer. The sphere has also been used as another model for the multidimensional aggregation of webrings or simply as a way to designate a kind of informational gravitation around a common orbit. The term blogo-sphere for example designates the ways in which all the personal web logs, or hyperlinked online journals, can be considered as ultimately related to each other within the same informational orbit of the blogging movement[3]. These figures are traced not so much by a link connecting two different sites across the grid of a common domain name, as by transversal movements, continuously spilling out of the grid, constituting the network as a space of centripetal and centrifugal movements, of spirals and vortexes, in various overall states of contraction and dilation.

While the topology of the web maintains a certain level of solidity that makes the notion of rings and spheres appropriate, the overall space of the Internetwork is also crossed by vortical movements that betray a microscopical fluidity and instability — informed by the power of rippling centrifugal and centripetal forces. A network microphysics is also made of temporary and unstable alliances and relations — such as the temporary chat channels that are opened up and closed down for the duration of a conversation or the fleeting email contacts that randomly link distant and even opposed areas of network space.

[...]

We also need to emphasize that while these centripetal and centrifugal movements are central to the evolution of electronic space, they do not take place within an isolated and self-referential infosphere. On the contrary, they are related the overall informational dimension that cuts across the global matrix of communication of which the Internet is part. As an open space, the Internet is not only open to the addition of new nodes, but also to the informational flows relayed by television, radio and popular culture, but also by political passions involving social antagonisms and conflicts. The centripetal/centrifugal movements that determine the fate of informational cultures are open to the overall plane of communication, and as such the Internet can be said to also be characterized by another movement, that which relates it to the various states of contraction and dilation experienced by the global communication system.

1-Gregory Bateson *Mind and Nature: A Necessary Unity.* (New York: E. P. Dutton, 1979), p. 174

2-See Janet Abbate *Inventing the Internet,* (Cambridge, Mass.: MIT Press, 1999)

3-See Rebecca Blood "Weblogs: a history and perspective" *in Rebecca's pocket.* (http://www. rebeccablood.net/essays/ weblog_history.html, (last updated September 2000; last accessed 22/04/03).

Think Twice

Matthew Fuller

"Thinking is like breathing you do it unreflexively or not at all. And if you happen to want to do it reflexively, or with full awareness, it becomes a full project of its own."[1]
Rosi Braidotti

Taking breathing seriously can be as simple as Marcel Duchamp's fine sentiment that "I like breathing — better than working."[2] It can become an enquiry into lungs, a song, a device to test air-quality, an aqualung or a method of self-treatment. Thinking about doing something whilst you are doing it, thinking about the way you think, reflexivity, is what the feminist philosopher Rosi Braidotti suggests takes something out of the sphere of a normal activity into the realm of being a "full project." By contrast, a normal activity is "understood" to the extent that it comes naturally, that it follows common sense, or is done in the way it's "always" been done. One thing shared by both science and art is that neither can rely on this easy understanding. They have to probe deeper, to ask questions, make trouble.

Thinking about breathing: thinking about breathing whilst you are breathing. This is a relaxation exercise, a way to get to sleep or to focus strength while giving birth. But thinking about doing something that you normally do unconsciously can create trouble. As an example, easy enough, try walking. Stand up. If you're reading this on a moving bus, even better. If you have legs, walk. But as you're walking take control of every muscle. Make each do its normal walking thing, putting one foot in front of the other, but with intent. Too slow? You fall over? Or more likely, you stay sitting. Keep reading — that walking's a tricky business.[3]

But is thinking simply about taking control? At a certain point, even doing the walking exercise, your mind has to give over control to the self-coordination built into those shapely legs of yours. Thinking has to collaborate with muscular capacity, bone, kinaesthetic[4] senses of position, capacity and movement. Dance of course is one of the arts which makes you think whilst you are walking. Every step is considered, planned or improvised out of a schema of available movements. But at the same time, a dancer learns the steps or movements enough to be able to remember them in the process of movement. One way of saying this is that they are rehearsed so that they don't have to be thought. But another way of saying it, perhaps more accurately, is that a context is made, the practice of dance, in which forces in the body come into dialogue with forces in thought and sensation. Watch, wait and sense what is happening and see what you end up thinking.

In one of a series of *Narralogues*,[5] in which fiction is combined with argument, the writer Ronald Sukenick poses in a different way the question of how to make a "project of its own" out of thought and bodily capacity. In writing, he argues, there is a tremendous energy to be found in what he calls, lifting a quote from the Victorian critic John Ruskin, the "innocence of the eye." Lifting from the Beats — poet Alan Ginsberg — he uses the idea of Wordsworth's "wise passiveness" to argue for a kind of receptiveness where the eye — the thinking, perceiving eye and mind combination – opens up. "When you're passive you see things others don't because you're more receptive, attentive." The "random, the accidental, the fortuitous" are trusted to move "beyond the stale, the static, the status quo version into a fresh view of experience." To become absolutely transparent, to mobilise this passiveness that Sukenick talks about is a skill akin to the dancer's. In order to dance in this way, in this way that is not a child's, in order not to have to think twice, one must have done so hundreds of times before. It must be learnt, but it is a question also of unlearning all that you thought could not occur in order to make oneself available as a site of experiment.

You may begin an experiment with a hypothesis, but must be totally open as to the results.

One of the powers of art is to make a project of thought and sensation, of bodily and conceptual capacity that is predicated on a fundamental investigation both of being alive, and of the world we are alive in. Allied with that it is also about making that world, of shaping and adding to it. Here, art and science have something of a common concern. Although they are expressed in different forms, (Such as calibrating the sensitivity of a sensor, calculating a norm for a set of control specimens, or developing a technique which adequately develops the arrangement of one set of matter, a chair in a room or a face, to another, a painter and his or her paints and canvas) they concern, in a certain way, the same fundamental problem.

The sociologists John Law and John Urry, express a similar set of concerns in their areas of activity, often in the study of science. Using Werner Heisenberg's proposition that, in physics, "What we observe is not nature in itself, but nature exposed to our method of questioning"[6] they suggest that, "Methods are protocols for modes of questioning or interaction, which also produce realities as they interact with other kinds of interactions."

This awareness of its own perceptuality, the way in which it sees things including its limits, has made the quantum physics of the kind that Heisenberg and others developed in the early parts of the Twentieth Century so enduringly fascinating to artists and others. Interacting with an interaction is not arbitrary, but about adding a reflexive process to something as it occurs. To do science or to do art is to construct an aperture into chaos. How that aperture is shaped will determine to some degree what kind of world reveals and makes itself through it. Further, what that aperture is connected to, which media,[7] what devices, what disciplines or movements, which kinds of cash flow or imagination. That is to say, you may be totally open to results, but use naivety only as a ruse.

There are easy to spot problems with some of the areas of science and art interaction. The most obvious are those cases where artists are there simply to illustrate or to make simple to a supposedly simplified public the nature of scientific ideas or results. Here, artists are used to be good at getting a message across, but blocked off from any fundamental access or capacity of thought or questioning. An equal and related problem comes from artists who take scientific methods and, in an arms race of obviousness, compete to be the first artist to use this or that scientific technique in an art context. One stands up and shouts for attention. "Look at me, Look. I'm the first ever artist in the world to design the first genetically modified this." You are a clever boy indeed. Other clever boys use art, the system of taste as a way of valourising their "necessary" cruelty. One stands up, "So yes, I may be doing marginally fruitless work on human neurology using the brains of live monkeys as pin cushions… But at least I use Mozart to drown out the noise of the drill."

In finding ways in which science and art might connect which are more than drivel or destruction it is possible that we might find people using methods derived from science and from art but in contexts which are not exactly either. Explicit Science and Art collaborations can be understood to be part of a wider field in which art and science are combined in lots of different ways "in the wild." One example of this is the immense amount of creative, campaigning and research work that has been developed in AIDS activism.

Thinking about your body working, how it goes on as a continuing changing, aging live process is something that often only happens when we step outside of the unreflexive state, when we become conscious that something is wrong, when we become ill. Thinking about breathing then takes on another nature, not just observing something occurring that you will do anyway, but becomes something of a question or of an assertion of resistance.

From the beginnings of the continuing and worsening AIDS epidemic, activist groups mobilised to demand access to drugs, research programmes and research design. In pioneer activist groups such as the network called ACT UP — Aids Coalition To Unleash Power —[9] much of the initial power of the campaigns came from the artists involved. They produced posters, graphics, and demonstration and campaigning techniques drawing on their skills and the ways of thinking and working they had as artists.[10] Crucially, they married these skills with urgent and difficult work gaining expertise in medical science. AIDS activists gained these from other movements, and from participants and allies inside medicine and other research areas. Learning to use archives, to read journals and to test and learn from the language and methods of science, at the same time as reflexively measuring them against the results in your own body and those of your friends is part of this movement, and continues to be so as it has spread around the globe. (A movement which as it has spread, takes on increasing amounts of the science, and more of the context in which that science is formed: including intellectual property regimes, relations between men and women, and the profoundly flawed global mechanisms for distributing wealth or resources and of rewarding research.)

Art and science collaboration "in the wild" have existed since both of these intellectual and practical currents emerged in the modern era. On of the means by which they have interacted is in the area of technology. Recently, attention has been renewed to the devices uses by artists to construct images.[11] In such narratives we can see how the "wisely passive" eye or the aperture into chaos is made. Such devices allowed artists to see the world and to the process of seeing in new ways. Realism, as in the precise supra-photographic paintings of Vermeer, only came into being by making vision technological. Sight sees itself in new ways by becoming strange, working through a grid, a camera obscura, or through lenses and other devices that make painting and drawing slow down, take notice of what had been missed.

Such use of technologies is often seen in contemporary art as being kind of naff. An over-involvement with technology and hence with technique is seen as denigrating the ironising reflexivity which the artist must take to their work. This irony is often what is used to differentiate art and science collaborations from both proper art and real science. Who after all

can imagine an ironic science? But following the Twentieth Century's cata-
logue of scientific horror, can there truly be a science of any other kind?

Marcel Duchamp, whose work, rather more often than his breath,
is called upon to validate this assumed disjuncture between conceptual-
ity and technique (in which the latter is imagined as simply the brainless
carrying out of work) provides one of a possible number of figures for
such a science. As art historian Rosalind Krauss puts it, such "cerebral"
uses of Duchamp are there to "purge it of its merely carnal connotations...
...ritually cleansed, transfigured, sublated."[12] One series of elements of
Duchamp's explicit, naff, precise, and addled programme of work operate exactly in the area of kinaesthetics. The series of Precision Optics
(1920, remade 1960) coupled retinal experience with the seeing acts of
the mind. An attempt on one level to see whether a mass-produced visual
gadget was a viable and humorous way of side-stepping the limits of the
gallery and collector system they were also a way of linking the carnal and
the conceptual by tricking the eye into seeing. Each of these Rotoreliefs
(1935) was a round piece of card with a series of circles printed round each
other asymmetrically. When watched spinning they appear to writhe, coil
and pump, making shapes that recede and protrude. The wisely passive
eye gets moist.

The cross-fertilisation of art and science is more profound and last-
ing than its sometimes gimmicky institutional blind dates can be seen to
acknowledge. Hawking the coupling as the ne plus ultra of innovative industry can do nothing except create a market for a spitoon for yawns.
Reflexive sciences and carnal, open-eyed and deliberating art however —
there's something worth practising breathing for.

1-Rosi Braidotti, Metamorphosis, towards a materialist theory of becoming, Polity Press, Cambridge, 2002

2-Marcel Duchamp, cited in, Marcel Duchamp, Museum Jean Tinguely, Basel, eds. Hatje Cantz Verlag, Ostfildern-Ruit, 2002

3-See the short story by Gustav Meyrink, 'The Curse of the Toad – Curse of the Toad', in The Opal and other stories, trans. Maurice Raraty, Dedalus Press, Sawtry, 1994, p.52-54

4-Kinaesthetics combines the Greek word for process and movement, kinesis, with aesthetics, that word which connects sensory experience to thought.

5-Ronald Sukenick, Narralogues, truth in fiction, State University of New York Press, New York, 2000, all quotes from p.67

6-Werner Heisenberg, Physics and Philosophy, George Allen and Unwin, London, 1959. Chapter three of this book, from which the citation is taken is also available online at http://www.marxists.org/reference/subject/philosophy/works/ge/heisenb3.htm

7-One of the advantages of the work of the work of the American group, Critical Art Ensemble is that they involve the mediation of science at the same time as they work on and in it, particularly in the area of biotech. See, http://www.critical-art.net/

8-Stefan Szczelkun, The Conspiracy of Good Taste, Working Press, London, 1993

9 Many ACT UP groups have useful websites. For example, ACT UP New York, http://www.actupny.org/

9-Many ACT UP groups have useful websites. For example, ACT UP New York, http://www.actupny.org/

10-A good deal of this early work is documented in Douglas Crimp and Adam Rolston, AIDS Demo Graphics, Bay Press, Seattle 1990. Reading through this book, one of course notes that Wellcome the company that developed the controversial and immenssely profitable AIDS drug AZT appears a number of times as an opponent of these artists and others using science. Their then chairman, Arthur Shepperd, now knighted, is named in one of the posters as an 'AIDS Profiteer'. The Wellcome Trust, a charity founded and funded by Wellcome plc, is the largest single funder of science art collaborations. Through the organisation sciart of which they are the sole funders (http://www.sciart.org/) they command a two-year budget of one million pounds for "the support and encouragement of innovative arts projects, which deal with biomedical issues."

11-See for instance, David Hockney, Secret Knowledge: rediscovering the lost techniques of the old masters, Thames and Hudson, London 2001 and, Philip Steadman, Vermeer's Camera, Oxford University Press, Oxford, 2002